THE LITERARY CONNECTION
VOLUME IV

AN ANTHOLOGY OF POEMS & STORIES

COMPILED & EDITED BY:
CHERYL ANTAO-XAVIER

Compiled and edited by:
Cheryl Antao-Xavier

Published by:
In Our Words Inc.
inourwords.ca
inourwords2008@gmail.com

ISBN: 978-1-989403-00-6

THEN
& NOW

INTRODUCTION

❖

As the submissions for *The Literary Connection Volume IV* came in, it was fascinating to see each writer's take on the theme 'Then & Now.' Reminiscing on defining moments in individual histories ranged from fond to quite disturbing. Whether couched in fiction or poetry or straight out non-fiction—the stories and perspectives show cultural diversity as well as the basic commonality in the human experience. Survival, making do, making sense of—we persevered, survived to tell the tale of how it was back then. In voicing our thoughts on the 'then' in the 'now' we learn and edify and move forward. The historical and emotional legacy of our past informs our present.

I am so grateful to the contributors for sharing memories, insight and perspective. It makes for enlightening reading!

I hope you, the reader, enjoy reading this anthology as much as I did.

Happy reading!

Cheryl

CONTENTS

Honey Novick

Honey Novick is a singer/songwriter/voice teacher/poet. A member of the League of Canadian Poets, she has been published in numerous magazines and anthologies. She has eight collections of poems including LyricalMyrical's *Ruminations of a Fractured Diamond*; Cancyp's *Monday Nights at the Butler's Pantry*; *Sanguine Encounters With Greatness* and the forthcoming *Undefeated Relevance.* She also has recorded eight CDs including *Rising Toward The Seraphim*; *Solid*; *New Songs for Peace* (a product of the UNESCO millennium endeavours), *Milton Acorn and The Free Speech Movement*; *Sal Mineo, My Friend, Elvis Monday Nights* and *Fat Albert's Coffeehouse artists*. Honey is an awardee of the 2017 Dr. Reva Gerstein Legacy Fund, as well as one of the Canada 150 Outstanding Neighbours for 'Liter-arti.' She has produced "Womanvoice" for 26 years. She is artist resource with the Friendly Spike Theatre Band, teaches "Voice Yoga" at the Secret Handshake Gallery, expressive writing at the Diane Frankling Coop and is a part of the Inkwell Writers and High Park Poets. Visit her at honeynovick.com

J. EDGAR

❀

J. Edgar"* is a movie showing on TV as I write this
I can't watch
It triggers a memory of a time my parents
took into our home a family of 4
husband, wife, son and daughter
they had no place to live
the husband had been imprisoned for his beliefs
served time, then released
we had them come live with us
not because they were communists (they were) but because
they were Jews

when they came to live with us my life changed (for the better)
these wonderful people were humanistic,
caring and never lost a sense of purpose
they didn't demean a child (me) nor disrespect
the differing opinions of my father
(who really didn't want them there but bowed to the demands
of the cost of living)
and now I'm reminded of those days
the days when I would peek out the window and
see men sitting in a sedan outside our house
day after day
when I asked my mother about this, she yelled
"get away from the window and don't move the curtain"
this is in my lifetime
I'm too young to have lived through
Nazi Germany and WWII but
I clearly remember McCarthyism in CANADA, I repeat in
Canada!!!
I fear we've gone back decades to those times
when it was prudent to get away from the window, not moving
the curtains

I thought we came a long way, baby
I thought that WWII was worth fighting for
fighting Nazis always will be
and here we are back again
same show, different players
reporters ordered from their jobs by a nation's president
a federal judge fired for forewarning the same president
he who offered to bring jobs back
Huh!!!
meanwhile Nazis march in Charlottesville, Va, 2017
costing the life of activist Heather Heyer
if you can't muzzle them, get rid of them
tear nursing babies from the teat of their mothers
rend families apart and send the children to
places where they will never reconnect
if women look too ugly put them somewhere they can't be seen
sell waterways and then poison them
give nothing for the poor
kill unarmed black men
accountability and the dignity of life be damned
oil is the commodity of the new holy grail
decency skewed
anything that can be sold, will be

when people fight and put their lives on
the line, they become visible
warriors don't always use physical force,
sometimes it's just determination
and ingenuity
these are current times
we've all been hacked, conned, trumped, played

cynical yes
hopeless not yet

* *"J. Edgar" is a 2011 film directed, co-produced and scored by Clint Eastwood. It stars Leonardo DiCaprio as the first head of the United States' Federal Bureau of Investigation who lasted for nearly 50 years. He was the most prominent anti-Communist in the USA (albeit during McCarthyism). After his death, it was revealed that he abused his power using the Bureau to harass, threaten and amass secret files and collect evidence using illegal means against activists, political dissenters and political leaders. Bibliography: Wikipedia*
On March 9, 1954, Edward R. Morrow wrote: "This is no time for men who oppose Senator McCarthy's methods to keep silent, or for those who approve. We can deny our heritage and our history, but we cannot escape responsibility for the result. There is no way for a citizen of a republic to abdicate his responsibilities. As a nation we have come into our full inheritance at a tender age. We proclaim ourselves, as indeed we are, the defenders of freedom, wherever it continues to exist in the world, but we cannot defend freedom abroad by deserting it at home."

Peta-Gaye Nash

Peta-Gaye Nash was born in Kingston, Jamaica, but has made Canada her home for over twenty years. A prolific writer, her first book was a collection of short stories titled *I Too Hear the Drums*, IOWI, 2010, revised in 2014. She has published six children's books: *Juliet Malevolent - An Evil Tale*, GMJ Creative Hands, 2015; *Essie Wants an Education*, IOWI, 2014; *Is Reine Still Sleeping*, IOWI, 2012; *Liam and the Lizard*, IOWI, 2011; *Don't Take Raja to School*, IOWI, 2011; *Where are Meadow's Manners*, IOWI, 2011.

Peta-Gaye won the 2015 Marty Awards for Emerging Literary Art and received an honorable mention for the same award in 2013. She won two Observer Literary Awards in her hometown of Kingston, Jamaica. A graduate of McMaster University, Peta-Gaye teaches English as a Second Language at Malton Neighbourhood Services in Mississauga, Ontario, where she lives with her husband Dominique and their four children.

She is currently working on her new passion—poetry, and another collection of short stories. She blogs on her website petagayenash.com and writes book reviews for Mississauga magazine *Community Captured*.

WATCH WHAT YOU SAY!

❀

January 15, 2015

The world cannot be a good place when preachy bosses like Melanie Kaur walk around all high and mighty. People say the end is coming, oh yeah, and I believe it too! Time was when a man could say what he thought. Not any more. Gotta watch what you say. All the f—in' time!

For years I worked in produce and was getting along just fine till the day I got a woman boss—a woman for Chrissakes!—and worse, an Indian! From then on had to watch what you say. She'd love to fire me, but she can't. Hah! She overheard me saying something and called me 'racist' and said 'my comments were inappropriate for the workplace.'

All I said was the truth… that there is no way in hell I would let my daughter marry a black man or a brown man or those religious crazies or any other of those immigrants swarming into the country. Wouldn't allow it. Over my dead body, I said. Then Miss High and Mighty walks into the lunchroom, listens to my *private* conversation and says, "Be careful what you say, Samuel, because I've seen it happen where that's exactly who your daughter will marry."

I laughed, made out like I thought it was a joke, but I said, "No Siree. It ain't gonna happen. Nope."

Might as well be honest. Why should I pretend to like what's happening to my country when I don't? Why be fake? But I said, "I have no problem with black people or any other people for that matter. I have no issues working with all kinds of people. I have a black friend. I'm just saying marriage is hard and you mix the race and it gets harder. That's all. I don't hate nobody."

January 20, 2017

This is the year I'm gonna find a new job. I say it every year, but this year has to be the year. I'm done working with

Miss High and Mighty. Sometimes I want to tell her to go back to her country. Back to the cane fields her family were cutting before Trudeau Senior let them in. She had the nerve to tell me I took 10 minutes extra for lunch. Bitch. I'm 63 years old and I've worked here for 30 years and she tells me I took an extra 10 minutes. She's a sick bitch alright. I'm thinking of retiring, just telling them to f—-k the hell off and drive Uber. The world cannot be a good place when a man can't have a shit at work in peace because he's rushing back to be on time. No Siree. My body ain't on her schedule. My wife Patricia says I shouldn't rock the boat so close to retirement but what do women know? Man's gotta take a stand, I say.

March 10, 2017

Son of a gun. Patricia didn't tell me that our daughter— my only daughter Claire—is dating a black guy! I am mad as hell. "He ain't settin' foot in this house," I bellowed at them. Patricia told me it ain't serious… but Claire is out every night. I hadn't noticed before because I was so busy with life and stuff. "How long has this been going on?" I shouted at them. Patricia said February. Claire said August. I said, "you mean like August last year?" She nodded and said I might as well know the truth. I glared at them. It's like my father always said, you can't trust nobody. Not even your own mother.

March 20, 2018

Claire looked beautiful. I've never seen her look more beautiful. My brother Mike came from Barrie. "So, what is that guy? Jamaican?" he sniffed.

"He's from Trinidad," I said.

"Trinidad, Jamaica, ain't it all the same?"

"That's like someone saying America, Canada, ain't it all the same," I said, annoyed.

"What's it like having a n—— in the family?"

"God, Mike. That's taking it too far. We don't use that word around here." What an ignorant slob. I looked around, worried that some of Anton's relatives or friends might have heard.

"Well whaddaya expect, Sam, we're all a bit shocked that this wedding is even happenin'. Can't I just ask my brother a question?"

"Ask all you want, Mike, but don't use that word in here. Truth is, I wasn't happy about it at first but then I met Anton. Man, I didn't want to like him, but he is funny. The man cracks me up. Then we sat down and had a few brewskis and watched some hockey and then the next day he had a barbecue. He can cook! He cooks a mean curry and makes the best jerk chicken. And he's making money at this new business of his, some internet technology thing. I don't know much about it, but Claire is happy. Sometimes, I think I like him better than her." I laughed so hard at my own joke that I choked, and Mike banged me hard on the back.

"So how much is this wedding setting you back?"

I looked around at the swanky decorations. Claire's dress alone cost six grand. The cake was two grand. I leaned forward and whispered. "Mike, I only had to buy this new suit and Patricia wanted that dress she's wearing. Anton covered the whole thing. It was the best news I ever heard." I slapped myself on the knee and laughed. "Best news I heard in a long time."

Mike looked jealous. He had his beady little eyes on me. "So the guy is loaded?"

"You could say that," I said winking at him.

January 20, 2019

I had the best news ever. It was right after the Mediterranean cruise Anton bought for Patricia and I. It was such good news that I wasn't cursing about going back to work. Claire is pregnant. Three months.

I was telling the guys at work. Man, I was saying, you should taste Anton's food. That man knows how to barbecue. He's a genius. The guys were ribbing me, telling me how I just eat and talk about the food and don't bring them none. I'll bring some for you mooches, I told 'em.

So then, I was telling them how Claire is expecting. Anton and I worried that if it's a boy, he might be, you know, one of them funny boys. The guys in produce were telling me not to worry, that my grandson wouldn't be no homo.

"I don't want no homo grandson," I said. "No Siree. It ain't gonna happen."

Then guess who walks by? Same old Miss High and Mighty. Always pokes her nose where it's not wanted.

"Still at it, are we, Samuel?" she says in her fake-sounding Canadian accent.

"My name is Sam and what do you mean by that, 'still at it'? I'm working as hard as any other guy here. I was putting the apples in place, taking the new ones and putting them at the bottom and the old ones on top."

"I'm talking about you saying inappropriate things in the workplace. We've trained you senior guys to not make comments regarding race, ethnicity or sexual orientation. I can't have you negatively influencing the younger employees."

"Those new boys are pansies," I said. "Always taking breaks. Something is wrong with the new kids comin' in. Those young guys act like homos."

"Samuel, Sam, be careful what you say because as I've said before, I've seen it where you get exactly what you say you don't want."

BETSY

Cousin Betsy from the country
with eyes green as the Caribbean shallows
that she waded into and never returned.
Green eyes so piercing, hard to forget
silently watched the world
inscrutable.

"Betsy was mad" they said.
I wanted to believe we all have secrets
that lurk in our minds.

And Gehenna exists in my mind too.
Cursed land, barren of joy,
where the light is blocked
by grey shadows.
Crisp air, red leaves
harbinger of winter,
weighs me down with pain.

Leaden limbs reach out for the sea
deep blue laps at my toes, my ankles
caresses my thighs
salt-like tears wrap my shoulders in warmth
"come in" she gurgles in my ears.

I, a water nymph like Betsy,
wade deeper into the shallows
never to return.

Bev Bachmann

Bev Bachmann taught high school English in the Toronto/Peel areas until she retired and began a career in writing. Her first novel *Christmas Touches* is available on Amazon in print and e-book format. Her second novel *Student Body*, a murder mystery set in a Toronto high school, is available at the Friesen Press Bookstore.

REMEMBERING NOVEMBER 22, 1963 — THE JFK ASSASSINATION

❈

I graduated from R.L. Paschal High School in Fort Worth, Texas in 1963 with every intention of continuing my education. Instead, however, I found myself living in Dallas and working in one of the downtown office towers that dominated the city's landscape. My existence was fairly functional and my days flowed by without much fanfare. However, one bright, beautiful morning in late November that was about to change. The President was coming to town.

It was around 11:30 a.m. that Friday when the entire staff in my office high-rise hurriedly evacuated the building. No one wanted to miss the show. I made my way over to where crowds of people were assembling on either side of the corridor through which the presidential motorcade was to travel. Being small in stature, I snaked my way to the front so that I could have an unimpeded view. With a little time to kill while waiting for the president's car to arrive, I scanned the crowds to see what kind of reception this Washington liberal, Roman Catholic president would receive in this right-of-centre, Republican, Southern Baptist bastion. After all, this was the birthplace of the John Birch Society. Amazingly, what I saw was nothing but eager faces glowing with anticipation. It was as if, politics be damned, everyone knew we were about to witness American royalty.

Suddenly a huge roar went up at the other end of the street and rushed like a wave towards the spot where I was standing. As the presidential limo approached, I realized I was standing on the side of the car where Jackie was sitting. As I watched, she craned her neck upwards and waved at the few people watching from windows high above her. I wondered why she was ignoring the wildly cheering crowd not more than arms' length away. But then I remembered I had read somewhere that John Kennedy had used the word "fey" to describe his wife. In any case, the woman was a stunner. I was struck by the fact that the shade of her lipstick was an identical match to the shade of pink in her pillbox hat.

But seconds were slipping away. Immediately I shifted my focus to the president. The first thing I noticed was that he was tanned and projected an air of vitality. The second thing I noticed was how handsome he was—much more so than on television. And unlike his wife, President Kennedy was looking at eye level at the hundreds cheering him as the slowly moving procession proceeded up the street. In fact, he continually turned his body from right to left so that he could engage with as many people as possible. And he was smiling—really smiling—from the heart and not just the face. I knew that I was looking at a man who was thoroughly enjoying himself. President Kennedy was having fun.

Then his car continued past me and he was gone. It all felt like a dream—a happy, lovely dream, but it was time to go back to work.

I had just arrived at my office building when I noticed a commotion at a co-worker's desk. Several people were huddled around a tiny transistor radio. Inexplicably, they looked stricken, so I moved in closer to hear what was going on. The news was one explosive shock after another. "The president has been shot." …. "The president has been taken to Parkland Hospital."

This last bit of information was almost as startling to me as the fact that he had been shot. Once, as a teenager, I had been a candy striper at Parkland and I saw firsthand how filthy and chaotic the place was. I remember, for example, if I was sent by medical personnel to another floor, I literally held my breath as I raced up and down the stairwells to avoid inhaling the fetid air. I saw written surgical reports that were blood spattered and I overheard interns making comments about patients that were decidedly disrespectful. And this was where the ambulance was taking the leader of the free world?

It didn't make any sense. Nothing made any sense. And then, finally the announcement: "President Kennedy has died." I couldn't believe it! Hadn't I just seen him half an hour ago? Wasn't he alive? And not just alive, but intensely alive? And now he's dead?

What did he do to deserve this?

We were told to go home. Silently we scattered. Somehow I found my bus, climbed aboard, and took a window seat. As we rolled along, I stared vacantly at the passing scenery. I saw men and women of all ages standing around like statues—frozen in place by paralyzing grief. Some were weeping. After awhile, I looked away.

Dallas had become a death zone.

It's hard to believe it all happened 47 years ago. Probably there are very few of us around today who were impacted so intimately by this cataclysmic event. And so the anniversary of Kennedy's assassination may not have the power to affect as it once did. I know that every November 22nd since 1963, I have stopped to think about the slain President and tried to honour his memory—out of respect, and yes, even affection. JFK wasn't a particularly great president. He had flaws, both personal and public. But what I saw on that infamous, unspeakably sad, day had nothing to do with politics or posturing or promises he was denied the opportunity to fulfill. What I saw was his humanity. And it touched my heart. It still does today.

Jason Chee-Hing

Jason (Wei) Chee-Hing grew up in the inner-city neighbourhoods of Toronto and attended all three universities in that City. Jason has very accomplished careers in both the public and private sectors and has varied interests. At the top of his list of interests is his love of literature especially poetry. Jason has been writing poetry for many years and his subject matter includes social justice, the human condition, relationships and nature. Jason will soon be publishing his first collection of poetry. This is his second contribution to *The Literary Connection* IOWI anthologies.

LAMENT FOR AMERICA

Jackboots on the ground!
I hear jackboots on the ground
That unmistakable sound
Of black polished leather
Smashing onto asphalt
That thunderous thud of spit-polished boots
Striking the ground in unison
Worn by young men
Idealistic young men
Who believe their cause to be true.

In far away lands they dream
Dream the dream
One day they will live in America
The American dream
The dream of free thought
Free expression
Rule of law
Where no one is above the law.

America what have we become?
Half-truths are now the truth
Truth shading is the *lingua franca*
Say it often enough
And the foolish will believe.

A populist leader feeds on the ignorance
Feeds on the baser instincts of men
There is mistrust and fear in the air
He spreads his gospel to the world
There are many takers
Goebbels you must be smiling
That evil smile
Somewhere in the afterlife.

America,
Land of the fearful
Fearful of the desperate from foreign lands
They want to live the dream
The same dream as our forefathers
Who themselves emigrated from foreign lands.

Jackboots on the ground!
I hear jackboots on the ground
That unmistakable sound
Of black-polished leather
Smashing onto asphalt
That thunderous thud of spit-polished boots
Striking the ground in unison
Worn by young men
Self-righteous young men
They believe their cause to be true.

We have forgotten the past
Or conveniently cast it aside
But I remember the jackboots at Kristallnacht
And I remember the jackboots of Il Duce
And the jackboots of Franco
And the jackboots of Peron.

Jackboots on the ground!
I hear the sound of jackboots
That unmistakable sound
Of black polished leather
Smashing onto asphalt
That thunderous thud of spit polished boots
Striking the ground in unison
Worn by misguided young men
They believe their cause to be true
Ready to stomp on the faces
Of anyone that does not look like them.

Jackboots on the ground!
That unmistakable sound
Much closer now
I hear jackboots outside my door
Are they coming for me?
Are they coming for you?

A BREATH OF FRESH AIR

Like a breath of fresh air
You blow into a stale dank room
Shuttered and still
As old as antiquity itself.

Your radiant smile
Lilting laughter
Innocent naiveté
Warms my heart.

For I am an old man
Hardened by life
Jaded by false pretensions
Served with a healthy dose of cynicism.

So keep on laughing
My lovely one
O that lilting laughter
And bring a smile
To an old man's heart.

I Said Hi.

I met you under a deep blue Caribbean sky
In a tropical land
Awash in lush verdant forests
Surrounded by azure waters.

I said hi
You stared at me
Asked why?
It is your eyes I said
Smouldering hazel eyes
As hot as the blazing sun
On my shirtless back.

Sparkling hazel eyes
That I got lost in
Helpless as a drowning man
In the deep undertow of an unseen sea.

Alluring eyes
Like a mystery
Whose story may never be told.

You blushed
When I said those things
But that made it worse
For I knew then
In that moment
Captured in your gaze
That I could never return
To my home.

Home, somewhere across the seas
Due north

Lands under an austere northern sky
Lashed by four seasons
Where trees lose their leaves
And the days get shorter
Where the sky
Glows at night
In iridescent colours
Of purple and green.

It is those hazel eyes
My love
That have kept me here
In your embrace
All these years
And, perhaps till the end of time.

A RIVER OF STARS

It is a clear crisp night
I feel the autumn chill
Snow will soon fall
As the seasons change.

It is a night of repose
I am contemplative
My restlessness has kept me awake—again
It is the infirmity of growing older.

Gazing at the heavens
I see so many stars
Like sparkling jewels
Set against a black void.

I see a river of stars
I see a milky cloud
Stretching from horizon to horizon.

Stars so close
I can almost touch them.
They gaze back at me
Like sentinels
From a distant past
So unimaginable.

I am comforted by them
Twinkling stardust
Like shimmering diamonds
Cut by a master
Who is not of this world.

Perhaps they will give me clarity
And ease my restless soul.

Seasons may change
But the stars remain constant.

WE WILL MEET AGAIN

We will meet again
It has been so long
Since we parted.
But I remember it like yesterday,
Some memories never die,
Never fade away,
Only to be cherished.

I remember when we were young.
We were children once
Shared every secret.
Promises were made
That cannot be broken.
That will withstand the test of time.
Even when we were apart,
We were near.

I know someday,
We will meet again.
The body never lies
When it shares intimate moments.
It makes a promise
That is seared in your soul.

We were once lovers
But life took us apart.
Your scent still lingers,
Like a fragrance,
So ephemeral,
But never forgotten.
Even as time marches by
We will meet again.

And like a pair of birds,
We will fly along the valleys,
above the rivers,
and into the mountains
as if we were one.

'Mute Swan Pair'
Photo credit: Merridy Cox

YOU ASK ME WHY?

You ask me why?
What is there to write about?
Why do you write poems?

I say,
Take a solitary walk
Along a winding trail.
Walk along the river
And hear the water gushing by.

At the break of dawn,
Watch the mist dissipate
Over a still silent pond,
As you hear the croaking of frogs
and bird song.

Stand atop the cliffs
And stare beyond.
And marvel at the vast expanse of water.

On a dark night,
Watch the full moon,
Pregnant and luminous
In all her majestic glory.

If you feel a sense of wonder
At these things
Then I write what you feel.
That is poetry.

'Egret on Driftwood'
Photo credit: Merridy Cox

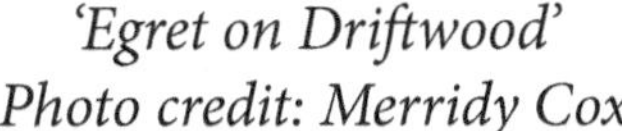

Jasteena Dhillon

Jasteena Dhillon is a professor of law and an international lawyer. She has a high profile in global media as an advocate for human rights in conflict zones. A graduate of the University of Toronto, she has an LL.B/J.D from University of Windsor Law School in Canada. She holds a Masters of Law in International Law from Leiden University in the Netherlands. She teaches Paralegal studies at Humber College in Toronto. She was an Associate Fellow at Harvard Kennedy School in the Carr Centre for Human Rights Policy.

Jasteena began her legal career as a children's lawyer for the Attorney General of Ontario. From 1998, she began an overseas legal advocacy career, beginning in South Africa. She went on to become an international legal and development expert in conflict, post-conflict and transitional areas around the world, including Afghanistan, South Sudan, Iraq, Sri Lanka, Indonesia, Bosnia, and Palestine, for NGO's, the UN and NATO.

Jasteena is currently writing her memoir, which focuses on the principles that inform her global work to protect the most vulnerable in conflict/disaster situations around the world.

RAPE IN BOSNIA—THEN & NOW
excerpt from an upcoming memoir

When international peace-time workers like myself go to conflict zones, we are directed to analyze root causes of the conflict in order to fix the long-term damage. For us, if we do that then *voila*, we build peace!

Not quite the case, as I saw a different reality when I went to Bosnia post-conflict as a Human Rights Officer for the OSCE. I thought of the ethnic cleansing and rape as a weapon of war as the 'root causes' of the Bosnian conflict. But when I opened the doors of my office, it was not these horrendous issues of brutality that flowed in as complaints. It was more of 'help me get my house back' or 'get a job.'

It is interesting how congruent people's actual lives are post-trauma to what it was before. Amazing how survivors of conflict in fact bounce back from horror to the mundane, even in situations like rape and move on with their lives—deal with history and recreate normalcy.

The brutality of the 1992-1995 war in Bosnia was devastating for its people, but I suppose normalizing what had happened during the war was the only way for the people to survive, move forward, and rebuild peace.

What really drove home this reality for me was the story of a young girl in a town called Derventa. I'll call her Lila to protect her identity. She was my assistant.

Lila had kind of frizzy, tight-curled hair, which was always a bit long and always in a ponytail—it sort of reminded me of an afro pulled up tight—very cool. She had very, very pale alabaster skin. I remember thinking 'what an unusual looking person in a beautiful way.' She was so striking. And again, just thinking of the insensitivity that we have when we do what we do—I never thought anything of us chatting about our lives. But one day, we did, and that conversation changed me forever.

I remember going with Lila after work to a café for

lunch and asking her where she lived. She said 'I live in Derventa with my mother. She is divorced.' I always assumed that wherever I go to work in conflict zones, the culture is always traditional. Something like my South Asian culture, where marriage is expected, and divorce is taboo.

But I knew from my research on the Balkans that the former Yugoslavia was cosmopolitan before the break up of the country, and divorce was not uncommon. We started to talk about each other's family and I remember asking Lila about hers, 'so who is your father?' and she said 'I don't really know. It is my brother, my mother and me.' It seemed like a normal conversation one would have even here in Toronto with a young person, where the parents are divorced, and the mother has remarried. But I could feel that there was something more.

As we continued to work together and have more informal conversations there were more and more pieces of the story that came out. She had been born in 1993, which means it had been in the middle of the war in Bosnia. Her mother was a Serb, she said. I knew that would be the case because Serbs lived in Derventa. But she said 'my father is Croatian.' As we continued to get to know each other she said 'but I don't know who he is. I think he was in the Croatian military.' And then I realized that the way women like her mother processed rape

With 'Lila,' just before leaving Bosnia.

is that they tell a different story to their kids. Her mother was likely raped by this Croatian soldier who had been stationed there during the war and as a result of it this girl had been born. And now the story is that 'your father is in the Croatian military and I don't really know who he is.'

What struck me about the story is not that the rape had happened, but that it is no longer an issue even for the victims and their families. It is as though people are not angry enough about it. It is almost like people accepted that it happened, and they moved on. They don't realize the deep trauma that it had for many of them. Lila's mother, I am sure, had gone through hell. She had been raped, she had a child and I remember Lila telling me that they are not in contact with her mother's family, because they didn't like her father.

I did ask Lila once 'do you want to get to know your father?' She said 'no, I forgive everybody for what they did in the war.' I remember her saying that a lot. She said, 'things happened, life went on and we have to move forward.' And I remember thinking that is how people are doing it. Not

At the OSCE office in Bosnia.

thinking about it. Whereas we in the international community are focused on the rape, the violence that happened to women as the main violation to address right away and with vigour—and it is right we should. Yet people there didn't seem to think that those cases were the priority in order to return to stability and peace.

In the West, we have the luxury of dealing with our trauma with the help of support and peace around us. They don't. For them—to build peace—life has to just go on. Once the war ended, Lila's mother had to focus on the immediate needs of her family, rebuild a house that had been destroyed, and find work. She had to live in a community which is now completely homogenously Serb because all the Croatians were expelled from the area. So, for her to focus on the fact that her child may be a child of rape of a Croatian military person, would have made her life difficult. So, she, and probably countless others, just put that horror that had changed her family forever far into the back of their minds—individually and collectively so that they can be peaceful and productive.

So, then I'm thinking, why am I surprised that this child of rape (likely), does not have that 'issue' as the focal point of her life? How else could she survive and live?

How did the mother cope? Her mother had said to her "your father was in the Croatian military, I don't really know him." And that was it. The girl didn't know a lot more of the facts. I felt like she didn't know who she was, but also that she didn't know how to ask the questions. She was in her early twenties and I wondered about her, as someone who advocated for women who have been violated. About whether as she got into relationships whether that 'issue' ever came out and negatively impacted her life.

But then I view things from the Western lens. That if this happens, you go for counselling, you re-live the situation, you get it out. Then when I see violence in those war situations—and this was not the only area where I saw it—I now just go: okay stuff happens, move on; we have to get peace and the larger community's health is at stake.

But I find it hard to forget these individual stories.

I wonder about them. I wonder if this young girl is still in Derventa. I remember her as being a very kind, compassionate woman. I always hope that she is okay, that she somehow got out of there. I have this fantasy that she got a scholarship and ended up going to Europe, then coming to North America to study, and getting her Canadian or American citizenship.

I hope she has.

Nina Munteanu

Nina Munteanu is a Canadian ecologist/limnologist and internationally published author of award-nominated speculative novels, short stories and non-fiction. She is co-editor of Europa SF and currently teaches writing at George Brown College and the University of Toronto. Her latest book is *Water Is…* a scientific study and personal journey as limnologist, mother, teacher and environmentalist. *Water Is…* was recently picked by Margaret Atwood in the NY Times as 2016 'The Year in Reading.'

In addition to eight novels, Nina—a writing coach since 2005—has published two books on writing *The Fiction Writer: Get Published, Write Now!* and *The Journal Writer*, Starfire, which are used in universities worldwide. Her upcoming novel *A Diary in the Age of Water* will be released in 2019.

www.NinaMunteanu.ca;
www.NinaMunteanu.me

COMING HOME TO WATER

❃

I was born in a small town in the Eastern Townships of Quebec, a gently rolling and verdant farming community, where water—*l'eau*—bubbles and gurgles in at least two languages.

I spent a lot of my childhood days close to the ground, observing, poking, catching, prodding, destroying and creating. Perhaps it was this early induction to the organic fragrances of soil, rotting leaves and moss that set my path in later life as a limnologist, environmental consultant and writer of eco-fiction.

My mother kept a garden in our backyard that she watered mostly with rain she collected in a large barrel out back. I remember rows of bright dahlias with their button-faces and elegant gladiolas of all colours, tall like sentinels. In the winter, my mother would flood the garden to create an ice rink for the neighbourhood to use for hockey. Somehow, I always ended up being the goalie, dodging my brother's swift pucks to the net.

Our dad frequently took us to the local spring just outside town. We walked a few miles up Mountain Road to an unassuming seepage from a rock outcrop with a pipe attached to it by the local farmer. I remember that the water was very cold. Even the air around the spring was cooler than the surrounding air. I remember that the spring water tasted fresh and that the ice it formed popped and fizzed more than tap water ice.

I followed my older brother and sister to the nearby forest and local stream. We stirred soil, flower petals and other interesting things with water to fuel "magic potions" that we inflicted on some poor insect. Yes, I was a bit destructive as a child—and I took a lot for granted. Like water. There was so much of it, after all. It was clean and easily accessed, fresh from the tap. We fished in the Yamaska River. We often went to Roxton Pond to picnic and swim. I was blissfully unaware of the scarcity of water in other parts of the world; that in many places women my mother's age and girls my age walked for hours to some dubious watering hole to gather water to cook and bathe with; or that within a short few decades some states in North America would make the collection of rainwater illegal or shut off the water to homes of poor citizens unable to pay their tax.

In the 1980s, I journeyed with my close friend Margaret to Tanzania, Kenya and Rwanda. We travelled with a small eco-tour company, camping and riding off-road. There, I met water scarcity head on. We had to conserve for drinking and bathing; most of us on the tour got sick from the local water. When I returned to Canada, I couldn't enter a mall or park—with its profligate displays and water excesses—without feeling shell-shocked. Africa had changed me. It had shifted my worldview and perspective forever. What I'd known intellectually, I now felt viscerally.

I was already pursuing a profession in limnology and began to write eco-fiction. Most of my stories explored dystopias of collapsed ecosystems based on humanity's lack of vision and respect. I became cynical.

When I gave birth to my son, Kevin, I felt a miracle pass through me. Kevin became my doorway back to wonder. His curiosity was boundless and lured me into a special world of transformation.

I took time off work to spend with Kevin when he was young. We went on great trips, from the local mall, where we had a hot chocolate and played with Lego, to the local beach on the Fraser River, where we explored the rocks. When he was no more than three, I took him on endless adventures in the city and its surroundings. We didn't have to go far. The mud puddles of a new subdivision after a rain were enough to keep our attention for dozens of minutes. We became connoisseurs of mud. The best kind was "chocolate mud," with a consistency and viscosity that created the best crater when a rock was thrown into it.

Kevin and I often explored the little woodland near our house. We made "magic potions" out of nightshade flowers, fir needles, loam and moss; we fuelled our concoctions with the elixir of water from a stagnant pool. This time the little insects weren't molested.

In 2007, I created my first blog, *The Alien Next Door*. It featured my observations and thoughts as a writer and aquatic ecologist. My profile recounted my favourite things; one of them was walking in the rain, hearing its rhythms and the smell of the Earth after a rainstorm. I was connecting with the liberating and energizing nature of rain and water vapour.

In truth, I was reconnecting with my own nature. And inhaling the scent of a shifting breeze. I would eventually transcend my traditional science; I would leave my hometown and my family to travel alone, meet archetypes who would lead me through swamp, quagmire and salty ocean, as well as crystal lake and rushing brook.

More and more, I've become fascinated by the interrelatedness of things in space–time, particularly in ways that can't be explained. Coincidence, precognition, déjà vu—these all appear to play a shadow-dance with each other. Quantum mechanics shows us that not only is "solid" matter made up mostly of energy and "empty" space, but also what makes a solid a chair (versus you sitting on it) is the vibration of its energy. Quantum science has demonstrated that light and matter are made of both particles and waves that can exist simultaneously. *Schrodinger's cat* is mystical and quantum entangled. That mystical cat braved the notion that particles can be linked in such a way that changing the quantum state of one instantaneously affects the other, even if they are light years apart. What does it mean when solid flows, ghost-like, through itself under certain conditions? In my trilogy *Splintered Universe*, one person's past is another's future. And where do they meet? Perhaps in dreams?

As a practicing limnologist, I examined water for its physical and chemical properties. Water was H_2O. I never thought to appreciate its quantum properties.

Water is the bold light of change. Water is the deep purity of soul. Water is who and what we are.

As we enter the seventh golden age, the nirvana of my soul consciousness rejoices with the water of my birth. All that we experienced since childhood has been mingled with the nature of our birthplace. Ultimately, we are connected in family and community through the watershed of our home. I will always feel connected to my birthplace. Its water is my water.

Now, as I roam the world as writer itinerant—travelling and teaching and learning—I find myself grateful for all that I have experienced and learned. Even the "bad" stuff, for even it has gifted me with blessings and opportunities.

Travelling the world has helped me realize that I was blessed with an abundance of water. I lived my entire life in a country of plentiful and healthy water. And for most of that time I didn't even realize it. Canada holds one fifth of the world's fresh water in lakes, rivers, and wetlands, as well as in our underground aquifers and glaciers. Canada's wetlands, which cover more than 1.2 million square kilometres, makes Canada the largest wetland area in the world.

Perhaps it is no coincidence that Canada is steward of the world's largest wetlands. Wetlands include marshes, swamps, fens, and bogs, all irreplaceable habitat for a huge diversity of nesting, feeding and staging waterfowl, reptiles, amphibians and mammals—many at risk. Wetlands provide a major filtration system, removing contaminants, improving water quality and renewing water's vitality; wetlands serve as reservoirs, controlling and reducing flooding toward a more balanced hydrological cycle. Wetlands are a source of oxygen and water vapour, serving a vital role in our global atmospheric and climatic cycles. As ecotones— transitional areas— wetlands protect coasts from erosion and provide exceptional opportunity for boundary interaction and the emergence of vitality. Like a good metaphor, wetlands "recognize" and encompass similarities between dissimilarities. Wetlands powerfully connect. Canada's strong multi-cultural policies and its open tolerance in embracing and celebrating diversity makes it the "wetland" of the world.

When I turn on the water tap in my house in Canada, it is pure drinking water. I don't need to boil it or filter it or test it for impurities and toxins. I am confident that it will nourish and hydrate me like water should. I can bathe without restriction. I can play with it.

My water hasn't changed; but I have. I do not take it for granted. I know that I am blessed.

I am home and I am so grateful.

Author's note: This story was first published in Gary Doi's In the Moment (*A Hopeful Sign*) Anthology, September 2016; *reprinted in* The Earth We Love, *anthology published by The Mississauga Writers Group, 2018.*

Author Nina Munteanu
photographed by Merridy Cox

David L. Tucker

David L. Tucker is an international award-winning television writer, producer and director. He holds a graduate degree in Fine Arts and is a professor of media. A former Associate Dean at Sheridan College and past Chair of the RTA School of Media at Ryerson University, David has been a frequent speaker at international arts and media conferences and has been published in scholarly journals. His short story collection, *One Way Ticket*, was awarded the Oakville Arts Council literary award. Best known for work on CBC's *The Nature of Things with David Suzuki*, David has garnered dozens of international television awards including a Gemini for Best Direction, and has presented his work at Hot Docs. He is a member of the Writers Guild, the Academy of Canadian Cinema & Television, and the Documentary Organization of Canada.

THE WAITING ROOM

❈

Ruben woke to discover he'd passed away during the night. A disconcerting start to his day.

At first, he wondered if he'd had a heart attack or stroke. There'd been no chest pains, dizziness or shortness of breath. Recent tests were fine, blood pressure excellent, heart strong, lungs at full capacity. He suffered from no chronic illnesses, apart from mild arthritis, hardly unusual for a sexagenarian. With good genes, regular exercise and healthy eating, he'd staved off infirmity better than most. His sudden demise made no sense.

Perhaps his doctor had missed something? But what? He'd spent his last days puttering around the house, a far cry from palliative care. Yet, here he was, pulseless, growing colder by the minute.

This can't be happening! A cruel joke? he asked himself.

A wave of anger washed over him. He felt cheated, his life cut short, lacking in sound and fury, signifying nothing.

A benediction of spring sunlight washed across his pale, unshaven face. Embalmed under his comforter, Ruben imagined the crocuses poking their heads up, below his bedroom window.

After Eleanor's death from cancer, Ruben had shut himself off from the world. But, today, it beckoned. He longed for a coffee. Maybe a caffeine jolt would raise the dead?

Lying prone on his back, Ruben gazed up at a large crack in the ceiling, a home repair left unfinished. The prospect of staring at it, indefinitely, felt cruel and unusual. To pass the time, he tried imagining it was the Sistine Chapel.

When was my expiry date, Ruben wondered? *When I ceased breathing three hours ago? The afternoon the car salesman directed me toward the full-sized sedans? Or the day those women joggers ran me off the sidewalk, like I was invisible?*

Ruben expected no one would call. His family and friends were mostly deceased, victims of old age, viral infections, heart failure, Alzheimer's, a traffic accident, a plane crash and a domestic tragedy. *At least, those deaths were explained!*

For sure, the postman wouldn't ring twice, now that they'd installed community mailboxes in his area. Neither would his self-absorbed neighbours. Most lived in newly-constructed monster homes, behind security gates and designer landscaping. Even the Jehovah's Witnesses had stopped knocking, considering Ruben a lost cause. He pictured attendants zipping him into a body bag, while a developer administered last rites at his front door.

Only yesterday, Ruben had rifled through old family albums, reliving happier times. Twenty years earlier, he'd been a television show runner, praised for his edgy characters and clever dialogue. Back then, he and Eleanor could afford regular vacations and dinners out.

Then along came Reality-TV, the Internet and social media, virtual reality and all the other media disruptors. Remunerations shrank and kids, fresh out of film school, jockeyed for screen credits. Ruben knew the writing was on the wall. A new generation of commissioning editors were taking charge. Ruben was yesterday's news.

He'd hoped for a send-off, some bit of recognition. But the world had no time for nostalgia, unless it could generate syndication rights or new viewers on YouTube. In this brave new world, Ruben found himself reduced to a mere avatar of his former self, left to wander augmented eternity.

Ruben could just make out Eleanor's French clock pinging quietly in the living room. His wife had discovered it at a local flea market: a study in alabaster, like her. Always a light sleeper, Ruben complained the ticking kept him awake. But after she died, he continued to wind it faithfully, his last link to her. Now he lay helpless, listening to it inexorably winding down, knowing that soon, she'd be lost to him forever.

Maybe in death they'd be reunited. That's always the hope, isn't it, the lost love, waiting patiently for a final, fatal Valentine? But Ruben lacked the necessary faith to pen any such narrative. He left science to explain the unexplainable and from what he'd read, life was just a collection of particles, expanding and contracting between atomic and gravitational forces. It was no place for reincarnates and resurrected souls. Or old men, for that matter.

Ruben had spent a lifetime waiting—first in cribs, then classrooms, on street corners, restaurants and hospitals. Waiting for dates, waiting to be served, waiting for change or simply waiting to go. Finally, waiting in this cold bed. But for what?

Ruben wondered what would become of all his cherished artifacts, marking a lifetime of consumption and achievement. Would Eleanor's clock get sent back to the same flea market for recycling? Would his press clippings and certificates find new life as compost? Could his awards tux and patent leather shoes sustain a homeless man on a winter's night?

At what point had their renovated Craftsman turned into an Egyptian tomb, a Home Depot crypt of household objects, complete with a fridge filled with Ensure, in preparation for the afterlife?

Ruben could hear Eleanor's clock strike six. *What happened to the day? Didn't I just awake up, sort of?*

Already, the sun was beginning to set, light fading into amber through the bedroom drapes. And still Ruben waited. He was reminded of an old Peggy Lee song. Is that all there is—that final disappointment?

The day had passed, like any other, bland as hospital food. At least there had been no pain, no poking or prodding, no need for bed pans or hospice care. He'd passed away quietly, no muss or fuss: a good death, according to most. Yet just as life had gone too quickly, so had death come too soon. To pass eternity, Ruben began dreaming up a bucket list of things he still wanted to do but now never would.

The next morning, Ruben rose early from his deathbed and headed for the nearest cosmic café, in search of a heavenly Cappuccino. He hoped by getting there early, he'd avoid a long wait.

❖

Lesley Strutt

Lesley Strutt is a writer living in Merrickville, Ontario. Her poems appear in literary journals, anthologies, and e-zines. In 2018, Lesley spearheaded the compilation and editorial of the League of Canadian Poets' special anthology on trees entitled *HEARTWOOD—poems for the love of trees*.

MORRIS

I was thirteen when the rebels came
skew chisel, parting tool
my parents   my brother   my sister   knife dripping

an arc of light cuts through cloud
in the distance two funnels of rain slash the ground
untrimmed   *shallow, steep cut, or straight gouge*

the sky is confusing with its different stories

I had to go but to camp they said   my
mind was a weapon they said
sent me back to do things   blood on the knife   my own people
all I had was violence   *deep gouge, bent parting tool*

the sky   nowhere to go   light slicing through clouds
flat chisel, hand forged, fine grained steel
between the maker and what's made

don't pity me   I've learned knives' pencil-like control
back-bent gouge, fine veiner, fishtail blade   I hold them
between the soft pads of my finger and thumb   and carve

heel of my hand pressing deep   what the world is made of
what we're all made of   buried in the fiber
brass ferrule   binding   strengthening this slender shaft

what it's joined to   the sky   different stories

Jasmine Jackman

Jasmine Jackman is a Vice Principal (Acting) and equity and social justice advocate. She is passionate about teaching culturally responsive and relevant pedagogy, volunteering, and working with youth in underserviced communities. She has been a teacher mentor, a facilitator of equity and special education workshops (at the school and university levels), a summer school assistant administrator and an active member on many community boards and associations for several years, aiming to bring about meaningful change.

Jasmine is the president of the United Nations Association Toronto Regional Branch and Regional Director for all United Nations Associations in Ontario. She is currently pursuing her PhD in Educational Leadership and Policy at the Ontario Institution for Studies in Education at the University of Toronto. Her research interests include: addressing social and educational inequalities in underserved communities, culturally responsive pedagogy, social and critical theory, race and ethnicity, teacher practice and mentoring for diversity and social justice.

GROWING UP BLACK IN TO—
BACK THEN

We arrived from England in the first wave of immigrants under the new Canadian 'race-free' immigration policy. My parents sought out housing in a middle-class neighbourhood despite efforts by their real estate agent to redirect them to rundown areas, with more 'people like them,' where they would feel more comfortable and housing was more affordable. My parents however, wanted us to grow up in a culturally mixed neighbourhood.

Soon after we moved into our house, I remember sitting on my stoop watching our neighbours moving out. As an inquisitive young girl of four years old, I innocently asked the man of the house why they were moving. He stopped what he was doing, put down the box that he was carrying, looked at me square in the face and said with unconcealed vitriol, "We don't want to live next door to a bunch of niggers!" I had never heard that word before. All I knew was that it wasn't a compliment. I just looked back blankly at my neighbour, picked up my jump rope and ran off to play with my friends. It would be some years before the meaning of that hated expression would become etched in my mind and seared into my soul.

We lived in a Maltese area in Bloor West, not too far from the Junction Triangle. Scattered among the Maltese families on our street were Polish, British, Dutch and Russian neighbours, as well as the lone Chinese family next door to us. It was a great neighbourhood. Everyone looked out for everyone's children and took great interest to ensure no one got out of line. You couldn't hide. There were many eyes watching you all the time. You really felt that everyone truly cared about each other's wellbeing.

One neighbour my age, Tony, decided to leave us a calling card a short time after we moved in. He shat on our front stairs right outside the main door to our porch. He wasn't too bright as he did the deed in broad daylight in sight of other children who were all too happy to inform my parents who had left the heap of warm human feces now circled by a family of flies. Well, my mom walked right over to Tony's house and let his parents know. His mother pulled Tony by his ear all the way over to our house to clean up his mess. I always wondered why he did it. Was he egged on? What was he trying to say? His misstep was soon forgotten and we became the very best of friends and were inseparable so much so that our parents would joke that we were husband and wife.

Our school had no people of colour and I was always the only black child in my class. I was good at sports so making friends was never a problem. I had three BFFs—Barb, Natalie and Rita. We called ourselves the Four Musketeers. We serenaded our teachers hello and goodbye like a barbershop quartet; we would walk home with them and even call on them in the morning. We would plan what we would wear to school the night before and come to school wearing the same things, such as jeans and pink tops or black pants and white tops.

Then it started. Grade Five. A petulant older boy by the name of Raymond took to chasing me around the schoolyard at recess or whenever he saw me, taunting me with 'nigger, nigger' and threatening to do me bodily harm. I complained incessantly to the teachers on yard duty and was repeatedly told "sticks and stones will break your bones…"—basically to ignore him. Raymond niggered and cooned me relentlessly for years.

By Grade Six the novelty of being the lone black person in my grade soon lost its shine. The warranty on cuteness and innocence had worn off. I was soon to learn that I was an interloper and that there were only Three Musketeers. Natalie, my BFF with whom I had been in every class from kindergarten to Grade Six, was having a sleepover for her 11th birthday. I had heard other classmates talking about the party and never once was concerned that she wouldn't invite me. We were Siamese twins attached at the hip. I instinctively felt the lack of invitation was just an oversight. Then after gym class in the presence of our other friends she said quite matter-of-factly,

"I guess you've heard that I'm having a sleepover at my house for my birthday." I was fully expecting her to say, "And you're invited!" Instead she added, "My parents don't want any black people at our house, so you can't come." She turned on her heels and went off with the other girls laughing and giggling about her party. It was like lightning had struck. The rose-coloured glasses disappeared, and for the very first time I finally connected with what being black and a nigger meant.

I don't remember crying or saying anything because I was stunned. What did all our years together mean? When I was younger, Natalie's mother would stroke my hair and smile and say something in Ukrainian, which I never understood but I always took to be complimentary—now I wondered. I was mad not at her parents but at my lifelong friend for not sticking up for me, for not challenging her parents' assertions. Why wasn't I good enough to sleep at their house? Did they think my colour would rub off on them? Did I stink? I never told my parents what had happened. My life took a 180-degree turn that day. From then on, I started to wonder if there could truly be a true

*Jasmine with her Mum and older sister in Toronto.
Photo supplied by author*

friendship between people of different races.

Some weeks later, I was waiting for the bus at Runnymede station with four male schoolmates following a track and field event, where I had come first in every event I had entered. Greg asked, "What do you want to be when you grow up?" John wanted to be a doctor, so he could look at naked women. Roman wanted to be an engineer and Greg an architect and Fred wanted to work in the foreign service as a diplomat. And then all eyes fell on me. "What do you want to be, Jasmine?" When I explained that I wanted to be a teacher, they all broke down laughing and John took the extra step of rolling on the ground, just to make a point. And finally, Roman blurted out through his laughter, "Well, if you are going to be a teacher then I am going to be the president of the United States."

I rode home in silence, the boys still giggling and jabbing each other about my ridiculous dream of becoming a teacher. I was puzzled. My marks were better than all of theirs. I was a straight A student in Grade Six. Why did they feel I was incapable of becoming a teacher? As the years passed, I started to pay attention to who my teachers were, who the principals were and then I realized. I had never seen, nor had been taught by a black person. Maybe I couldn't be a teacher. Maybe black people were not smart enough. My self-esteem plummeted.

A short time after, the gym teacher, who looked like a member of Air Supply with his strawberry blond, shoulder-length hair coiffed and feathered perfectly and with his sunburned freckled skin, had us sitting in a circle in the hall as we waited for our chartered bus to another track meet. He started going around the circle asking people various questions like, "Where are you from?" His finger landed on me. I responded I was born in England. He waved his hand back and forth impatiently as if to erase writing on a blackboard and said, "No, no. There are no black people in England. Where are your parents from?" This would become a familiar reframe I would hear time and time again throughout my adult years.

In Grade Seven I was put in a split 7/8 class with five other Grade Sevens. We were all friends and excellent students.

I missed a lot of class due to volleyball, basketball, track and field, cross-country and the odd drama practice. But I never let my school work slip. I was very shy. And being in a class with girls with Dolly Parton breasts and boys with beards was very unnerving. All of the Grade Sevens scored relatively the same on tests and were very competitive. So when I received my report card I was very shocked to see that I had received Ds in math, reading and science. I was devastated. I had never received anything lower than a B+. I was really puzzled. At parent-teacher night, my teacher suggested to my mom that I should be kept back a year and that my parents should consider sending me to a technical high school to learn typing so that I could move right into being a secretary after Grade 13. My teacher had already shipped me off to technical school in her mind. The colonial mindset had told my mother never to question a teacher's "good counsel." It was my older sister who reminded my mom that I had just left Grade Six with straight As and that clearly something was not right, and she should fight to see that I was put ahead. So, the teacher reluctantly passed me on to Grade Eight.

From that date on I wanted nothing to do with typing (I still can't type). I also decided that my sports and extracurricular activities would have to be curtailed significantly. I remained captain of the volleyball and basketball teams but pulled out of many track and field sports, even when the principal and gym teacher tried to convince my parents to send me to run professionally. I refused. I was a gifted athlete, but sports were not my first love. I didn't want to be known as a jock; I wanted to be educated—well educated. I wanted to prove to those boys and myself that I could be a teacher.

My younger sister and I took piano lessons after school and one day in Grade Eight as we were leaving the schoolyard an hour past the end of school, Raymond, my lifelong tormentor, lay in wait for us with his even more delinquent brother. As we made our way across the expansive yard, they appeared from out of nowhere wielding a jackknife, jabbing it in our faces, waving it menacingly, threatening to cut our "fucking nigger throats." This is where I put my track skills to the test. I told my sister I would get help and sprinted past the mad boys with my sister running behind me and the two older boys in tow screaming, "Nigger, you're dead." I ran into traffic to escape them and sprinted for my life. As fate would have it, my mom was on her way home on the bus riding by the school at that exact moment. She was standing up getting ready to disembark at the next stop but got off one stop earlier when she noticed that we were being chased by two boys. I literally ran into the arms of my mom, almost knocking her down. When the boys realized we knew her, they took off. We told our mother what had happened and she walked back to the school with us to speak to the principal, Mr. Arnold, who was all too willing to give her the students' parents' phone numbers and addresses. I don't know what my parents said to their parents, but the taunting stopped. Even today I wonder what these boys might have done if they had caught us. Would they have slit our throats? Why did they hate us so much? Was the colour of our skin so revolting?

In Grade Eight I studied every day. I became so nervous—nauseous even—about taking tests because I felt they would reveal that I wasn't good enough—that black people were stupid. After all, I had almost failed Grade Seven. I remember our first geography test. I rewrote my notes several times, memorizing the bolded definitions verbatim in our textbook. And to my delight, our test was made up mostly of the bolded words, so I easily completed the test. I knew I had a perfect or close-to-perfect score. I was so relieved and convinced that things would fall back in order. Until the next day when the teacher, Mr. Collins, called me to his desk. He handed me my paper which had a big red zero at the top and he scolded me for cheating on the test. He didn't allow me to speak so that I could explain why my answers were exact descriptions as found in the book. His logic was ridiculous because I sat at a desk attached to his with five other students. Surely if I had cheated, he would have seen me. The lesson I learned that day was, I better not do too well on tests and assignments because the teacher would never believe it was my own work and thus accuse me of cheating.

At the beginning of track season, I proceeded to the gym to sign up for one or two events only to find that the gym teacher had signed me up for several more. I was furious but too shy to complain. I complained bitterly to my friend, Mary. She went directly to our home room teacher, Mr. Collins, to explain the problem. I was so surprised that Mr. Collins took me with him in tow to see the gym teacher to demand that I be removed from the events I hadn't picked. That was the first time in seven years that I had decided to only do two track events— 50-yard dash and relay. The gym teacher wasn't pleased and the way she showed it was by giving me a D in gym. But just to make her point, at graduation, the Athlete of the Year Award was given to a girl who had just come to the school the year before. Several teachers approached the gym teacher at graduation to inquire why I didn't get the award. The gym teacher came up to me and whispered in my ear with a smirk on her face, "If you had been more cooperative it could have been yours." There were no tears, just the sad realization that life was not fair.

As a young child I never wandered around contemplating the colour of my skin and the many barriers I would have to overcome because of it. My parents never told me, "Look, people are going to treat you differently because your skin is darker then theirs," or that they would challenge my intellectual ability, believing that I was only good for sports and dancing.

I was saddened because what could have been a great memory of my childhood would always be tainted by the actions of a few people. Today, I look back at the many incidents that could have sent my life onto another trajectory, but because of good people, family and friends, I was able to overcome setbacks, regain my belief in people and learn to navigate a system that fails to acknowledge racial inequality in its practices and policies.

It is true that God always ensures good people prevail.

Lindsay W. Albert

Lindsay W. Albert, an avid reader since pre-school, began writing at age 7. In 2013, Lindsay launched herself into the Mississauga literary scene and her poems were published in two anthologies. Lindsay has been a contributor in several *In Our Words Inc.* anthologies. She was a Feature presenter at the *Oakville Lit Café* (2015).

Recently, Lindsay diversified her creative expression to include photography. Lindsay's writing and photography have been published in two issues of *The Artis* literary magazine, in one of which she was a Featurette. She is dedicated to bringing healing and inspiration to her audience.

TREE OF LIFE

❁

Beloved sister
No growing up together
at three months eight days
you were laid in your grave

Next to your grave
a small pine tree
unknowingly served
as a marker to
your resting place
and passing time

Annual visits to
your small flat stone
to trim 'round the edges
where grass has grown
Presence of life mixed
with presence of death

Sixty birthdays pass
Your pine tree towers
Its boughs spread wide and
scarred by the weather
still stands as marker
of both place and time

I've felt my grief change
In my heart you're nigh
As long as I live
your story I share
Love and grief, too,
will not ever die

❁

Pine tree 'marker'
Photo submitted by
author

RESILIENCE

❋

Raging waters
pummelled
shorelines and walkways
as the lake regurgitated
trees, rocks and debris
from its depths

Breakwaters submerged
Vanished
Meant to protect
now rendered useless

Waves crashing
Relentless
Concrete slabs
torn from their rebars

Iron railings
Mangled
Ripped from
cement foundations

Boulder peninsula
Swallowed
by the surf
Hundredweight logs
heaved onto land

Credit River rises
Oblivious
to embankments
meant to contain
are instead immersed

Torrents of rain fall
Incessant
though drenched grounds
can hold no more

Storm passes, skies clear
Relief
not immediate
Water levels recede
in Nature's own time

Assessing aftermath
Damages
born of the storm's
vicious rage

Healing begins
Revealing
with new knowledge
strength and wisdom

Redesign and rebuild to
Withstand
future storms
that surely will come

This is
Resilience

❀

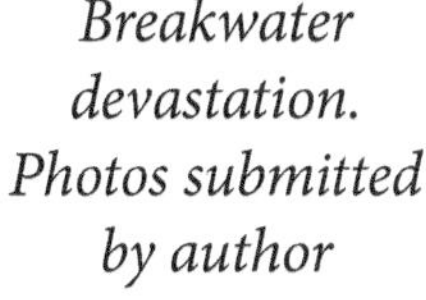

*Breakwater
devastation.
Photos submitted
by author*

Cheryl Antao-Xavier

Cheryl Antao-Xavier is a published author of two poetry collections: *Dance of the Peacock*, IOWI, 2008, and *Bruised but Unbroken*, IOWI, 2017; a children's book series *Welcome to Maple Woods*, IOWI, 2012; and a guide for writers *Self-Publishing the Professional Way!*, IOWI, 2018.

Cheryl has had a 30-year career in the publishing industry in positions ranging from author, editor, proofreader, desktop designer, and publisher. She has a Bachelor's degree in English Literature and has honed skills in writing, editing, and publishing at Ryerson, Toronto. In 2008, she set up In Our Words Inc., a publishing company, and to date has published over a hundred titles. In 2017, she set up a non-profit organization RISE Up! Rise ABOVE! (RuRa) to promote reading and creative writing.

THIRTY YEARS CANADIAN

A score and ten
from then to now
        shifts on every level—
dark chips in the mosaic
        polished to fit
in the big collage.

No longer the outsider looking in,
        chafing in ill-fitting shoes.
Stand in a new sense of self—
sift through old, blend in new
prospect and promise
offspring birthright.

A banner once seen from afar
        a symbol of safe haven, free
promise to those with means
and those in need.
A welcome not with melting pot, but
an umbrella of many colours.

A score and ten seems like forever
        to wind one's way home.

STREETSVILLE

Old tombstones in this cemetery
date back two centuries—
their epitaphs face Queen Street.
A spirit of yesteryear hovers
over this reluctant city,
always a village at heart.
What was it like in their day?
What would they make of Streetsville today?
Questions flow, caressing weathered stone
with an apology…
forgive the clamour, fumes, raucous trade.

Fresh eyes take in a century of culture
lovingly preserved.
What will it be like two centuries hence?
Questions flow, caressing weathered stone
with a prayer…
let us remember, cherish, honour.

UNCLE GEORGE & THE ANGELUS

❧

He stopped at the sound
of the *Angelus* bells
reciting

Angelus Domini nuntiavit Mariæ.
Et concepit de Spiritu Sancto.
Ave Maria!

He stood to attention
hat in hand, head bowed
whispering the *Angeles* prayer.

Behold the handmaid of the Lord.
Be it done unto me according to your Word.
Hail Mary!

His cotton suit wrinkled in the summer heat,
his collar threadbare,
tie limp from a thousand knots,
shoes patched, re-patched and shined,
cataracted eyes blinked behind thick lenses,
sagging jowls worked to sound out
the *Angelus* prayer.

Et Verbum caro factum est.
Et habitavit in nobis.
Ave Maria!

The memory of him standing
at the corner of Mansfield and Wellington
arouses memories of a gentler time.

I hear the *Angelus* bells ring no more in that town
no one stops to whisper
the *Angelus* prayer.

Pour forth, we beseech thee, O Lord,
Your grace into our hearts…
Glory be to the Father!

My child does not know what 'Angelus' means
I had to look up the words myself.
Once recited in Latin in Uncle George's day,
in English in my days,
no more in my child's days.

Today, at the corner where Uncle George had stood,
no belfry call could pierce Saddar's noonday clamour.
No one recites the Latin *Angelus*
and few the English version.
The bells of old St. Patrick's Cathedral
where Uncle George and his generation—
were baptized, married and eulogized—
are now silent at the *Angelus* hour.

May God's help be with us always,
and may the souls of those who died in faith,
through the mercy of God rest in peace. Amen

❁

SHADOWS

caught a glimpse of her old self
in her eyes
behind the shadows
but she's different
from the picture—
of three decades ago—
that I place between us
caught in 'crazy' pose
so carefree, so ambitious
so long ago

our eyes lock
the shadows mirror
over rueful smiles
both think it
both know it
if we could go back in time
fewer shadows would shade
fond reminiscences.

Merridy Cox

Merridy Cox has published poems and photographs in *Scarborough Fair II*, *The Literary Connection Volumes I, II, III and IV* (with photos), and in *The Literary Gourmet Revisited*. As editor, she has published *Themes from A Course in Miracles: How Brothers Can Get Along* (with photographic illustrations) and annotated and published *Edwardian Pets and How to Keep Them* (by Frank Finn, 1907). She has written a booklet, *Nature Breaks for Busy Urbanites: Five Doses for Relaxation* (with photos). In other work, she has copyedited *Water Is... The Meaning of Water* by Nina Munteanu and *Beast Master* by Janice Graham-Foscarini.

THEN AND NOW

I yearn for yesterday.
It seems so unfinished.

Back then, I didn't drink coffee—
I just lived.

Maybe now I'm old enough
for a sip of wine.

I'm addicted to tomorrow…
I taste my want of it.

Today, I get up—go, go, go, go…
Where are the roses?

My feet take me to the water.
It's flowing still.

I look up and there you are,
down by the bridge.

❁

UNCOMFORTABLE SANCTUARY

In a hill of rock created
by some slow, glacial movement—
an anomalous formation,
a cubic space—an open box,
a rock-walled room with a sky roof—
a secret place for sunbathing
full of cricket sounds and bird song,
a quiet place for reading books.
Pine needles and grey lichen—
uncomfortable remoteness:
the introvert climbs out, homebound.

craving aloneness
she searches sheltering rocks—
prickly pine needles

BIRDS

a large gnat flies
slowly by my window…
kinglet snatch

flash of colour
small bird
lost in leaves

'Damsel Fly'
Photo credit: Merridy Cox

FAMILY

my father practised
a chickadee's whistle
he calls me yet

Granny knit, Mum knit
my legacy
hand-knit

HAIKU FOR EVENING

moonless sky
drowsy eyes
monkey brain

half moon sails
towards
a star

book pages
turn lazily
from dream to dream

listening
distant chimes
awake me

full moon skips
across the sky,
hunting stars

I.B. Iskov

I.B. (Bunny) Iskov is the Founder of The Ontario Poetry Society, theontariopoetrysociety.ca. Bunny has won a few contest prizes and she has several poetry collections. In 2009, Bunny was awarded the R.A.V.E. Award by the City of Vaughan as Art Educator/Mentor in the Literary Arts Division. She is the recipient of the Absolutely Fabulous Woman Award, Arts & Culture category, 2017.

BEFORE THE FLOOD

❁

Once, when the earth was young
and Eden just a garden,
the names of clouds were only a sigh.

Once, when the smallest shiver
wafted through autumn,
a fashion statement resonated in basic green.

Once, when no shame and life

were contained in a breath,
each moment ignited in a glimpse
between mouths full of fruit.

Once, while everything still
was fresh and naïve,
the twilight brimmed a rainbow
of benevolence and gold.

Once, when my man was just a boy
and terror a horror movie,
each peace protest from a flower child
sang a new era.

Once, when buildings were giants among men
and the telephone a dynamic lifeline,
gentle shadows hushed a tableaux of fury
between flightless flora and fauna.

Once, when beasts were confined to zoo cages
and communism the perfect enemy,
rain-soaked and dramatic
iron fear curtained a new born question.

Once, when snakes could walk the earth
and apples promised wisdom in a bite,
the air harnessed
a rhapsody of fire.

(Runner Up in *Voices Israel 2008* Anthology); First published in
Sapphire Seasons, Aeolus House, 2010

ALMOST PERFECT

My life began
in the cradle of a star
on cloud oceans

I was the goddess
of wild orchids
wrapped in amber sun
flawless   almost

Unblemished
in the high chair
like the sun
head bent under heaven
my world tilted
the axis the vision
seen best with one eye

Dubious growth
under one side of my jaw
stunted connections

I should have held my head
up straight,
the world looked better
from clouds   almost
perfect sideways

First published in *Sapphire Seasons*, Aeolus House, 2010

MARTIN'S CHILDHOOD

❉

Even as a young boy,
Martin had a penchant for guns.
At the tender age of five,
he wore his cowboy outfit proudly,
holding two pistols – one in each hand.

All the gold in the world
could not match the wealth of power
gifted to him in those revolvers.
He was both hero and villain,
both bully and protector.

His past rushed through time,
as he leapt from child to man
at that tender age of five.

He was no longer the cherished baby.
A new sibling stole this starring role.
His new star was that of SHERIFF,
worn on his chest, concealing a wounded heart.

Both mother and father were far too preoccupied
with their jobs, leaving the care of his baby sister
in his small but capable hands,
already filled with marbles and comic books.

His boyhood friends, busy with playing tag
and baseball, soon disappeared.
There was no place in their games
for this little man,
burdened with a baby sister.

Resentment fell into a tiny place in Martin's history.
Only guns remain his source of joy.

First published in *Martin's History*, Beret Days Press, 2013

TESTING THE WATERS

*In memory of Heine Mondrowitz, who drowned on Lake
Nippissing on Aug. 21, 2006*

It is not hard for me to remember you
scanning uncharted territory.

Others, far less adventurous,
stood land-locked at dance-floor edge
while music flowed anxious and free.

At twelve, I had only started to develop
a love for music and dancing
and you   my first crush glided
across the endless sea of grey-blue floor
and asked me to dance.

Sadie Hawkins would have been proud.
It was my day and hers.
When you sailed me
around and around,
judges were pointing
and gave us high marks for showmanship.

As our ship reversed, we twisted in open water.
I think this happened when you died.
You spun around and around on a windy axis,
burned into sunlight, and sailed away to heaven.

❀

First published in *Sapphire Seasons*, Aeolus House, 2010

NEGATIVITY NEGATED

❁

My bitter experiences
have left me
in that hollow nest,
deep and tough
high above tempests
hatching eggs of wisdom.

Once upon a time,
I searched for the perfect port.
When I opened my hands,
flies and wasps caressed naïve palms,
and my dream of finding solid judgment
turned into a nightmare. Rough
reality slapped me hard.

I turned into liquid,
flowed into a sea of forgetting
and spawned my own memories.
I hid my tongue amongst reefs,
distanced my voice like a night star,
doctored my stung poems
with salt and sympathy.

I discovered there is no happily ever after,
only an ever after with conjured
and crafted words –
words that can heal the mind
and the pain.

First published in *Sapphire Seasons*, Aeolus House, 2010

GLASS HOUSE

Sunlight falls on dusty shelves.
One silver goblet begs for shine.

Candlesticks, erect as sentries,
guard the precious paradise.

I open my cabinet doors,
rearrange familiar figurines,

hide what's missing,
chipped or broke.

I care for moments,
dust them off, display them
on little easels.

I'm composed.

Previously published in *Skirting the Edge*, In Our Words Inc,
2015; *In A Wintered Nest*, Serengeti Press, 2013; *EnCompass 11*
anthology, Beret Days Press, 2013

WHERE IS SHE?

Half-smiling, a young woman stands in sepia tones,
her light brown hair coiffed like Garbo's.

My mother, in her better memory, confessed:
This is my sister, Basha. She was my father's favourite.
Isn't she beautiful?

My sixteen-year-old brain racing,
I wondered why
my mother never told me
about this other auntie,
about her husband,
my other uncle
and their two daughters,
my other cousins.

I wondered why
I never got to visit them
and why my mother's parents never mentioned
this important person,
their eldest and most attractive, intelligent daughter,
all the years they lived in Canada
after the war.

I looked at my mother full of questions
and asked only one:
Where is she?

My mother, wiping tears, blurted:
She was murdered by the Nazis with her husband and children.

First published by *The Passover Literary Supplement of The
Canadian Jewish News*, March 2013

After I Was Born

In the oven-warm delivery room,
bread-flesh came away
body hairs gold as challah.

Impossible contradictions paint my skin
between existence and enchantment
sweep years coagulated into colours.

These colours change.
I sometimes forget
they're framed in stained glass.

White only lives for the winter
among dead roses, scrawny trees.
Poems too shed their meanings
like leaves on sallow parchment.

In the family of loud summer
red bursts into watery flames,
stains the walls of my heart.
Turns grass to blood.
Turns sky to blood.

As I grow old the seasons elude importance.
Fog and fire co-mingle reluctantly.

Every time I shed skin
I am caught off-guard.
There are always shades
of indifference.

First published in *Sapphire Seasons*, Aeolus House, 2010

Susan Ksiezopolski

Susan Ksiezopolski is an award-winning published author, speaker, coach and facilitator. Her work has been featured in various anthologies, magazines and on-line platforms. In 2018, Susan founded WriteWell, supporting organizations and individuals to unleash the creative power of writing to create a path to success and wellness. A graduate of the Humber School for Writers and a Lead Training Facilitator with Toronto Writers Collective, Susan developed and delivers The Writers Workshop across the GTA. She also facilitates workshops for the Toronto Writers Collective, giving voice to marginalized communities. Visit her website mywordsnow.com.

PAST PRESENT FUTURE

Holding on to the past
Can't save me from the present

The present still comes
Unrelenting
Exposing
That which has no answers
Making
The future seem further
And further away

Letting go of the past
Can't save me from the future

The future still comes
Ready or not

Holding on letting go
Twirling into the unknown

The dance of past, present, future

Whirling in my head
Destroying past
To save the future

Keeping me still
In the moment
Holding on to myself

UNRAVELLED

Ripples of tomorrow
Crowd out yesterday
Waiting in the wind
To arrive
Waiting for the wind
To carry away
Yesterdays unravelled
Jigsaw edges
Ripping apart
Hearts held in silence
Now resting
In a stream of hope
Under the bright sky
Burning away
The sins of yesterday

Retreat
Into the now
Waiting in the wind
To arrive
Waiting for the wind
To pull you in

Today effortlessly floating
Into the now
Out of yesterday
Building tomorrow

Shimmering in the sun
Caressed by the shadows
Dancing at my feet
In tune with life

Yesterday retreats
Leaving the space for
Now to fully arrive

Drowning in the dazzling sun
With room to expand into
The day until tomorrow comes

'Toronto Old, Toronto New'
Photo credit: Merridy Cox

WHERE I COME FROM

I come from two countries
A long forgotten one
And this not my native land
Always feeling torn
Where is it I belong?

An atlas on my lap
Spinning
Places visited
Places dreamed of
Places lived in
Homes now forgotten
Left behind
Like dishes
Leaving a dusty trail
Of days gone by

Days wondering
Where on earth do I go?
Why on earth am I still here

Choices to be
Anywhere on the globe
And yet rooted here in this place
I wasn't born – always torn

'Toronto Old and New'
Photo credit: Merridy Cox

Wayne Croning

Born and educated in Karachi, Pakistan, **Wayne Croning** immigrated to Canada in the early 1990's. In *Karachi Backwaters*, he writes of his passion for the sea, boating and fishing. He has written several short stories, two of which were published in a magazine called *Anglos in the Wind*. He has also co-authored two anthologies.

Wayne lives in Winnipeg with his wife and two children. History, boating, reading and writing are his main hobbies. He is currently working on his second book.

REMEMBERING MRS. MARTIS' TIFFIN

❀

After my grandma passed away in the early 1950's, grandpa had to make food arrangements. He decided to arrange a 'tiffin' (a 3-4 tiered metal food container) with food from the kitchen of Mrs. Martis, who was in the food catering business, to be delivered daily to his home in Chand Gulli.

Mrs. Martis' home was a ground floor apartment just a few lanes away in the heart of Saddar. As soon as you entered her kitchen, you were pleasantly engulfed by the aroma of freshly cooked curries. A large gas stove dominated the kitchen and a concrete countertop is where food was prepped and later sorted out for delivery. She had a tiffin-walla on a bicycle who would come by just before lunch time, pick up several tiffin containers filled with food and deliver it to various homes and offices in the Saddar area and beyond.

As per my mother, there were two tiffin container runs for grandpa's home. One was in the afternoon where lunch was dropped off; the tiffin-wallah would then pick up the empty (clean) one and take it back to Mrs. Martis's home. Later in the evening, dinner would be delivered and the (cleaned) lunch container would be given back the next day. A perfect set up!

My mother adds... "Lunch usually consisted of rice and curry; different ones. Some days, just meat and potato, some days *daal* and other times a veggie dish. There would also be a side dish like meat cutlets (kababs), which usually came with the daal and rice. On Friday's there would be fish curry and rice with fried fish, which was mostly *Surmai* (King fish). In those days, the fish was fresh and very tasty. Sunday's was a special lunch; usually fried rice like a pulao or yellow rice with chicken curry or kofta (meatball) curry. Dinners were mostly always with soup, bread and some dry dish like meat and potatoes with carrots and peas. Dinner also usually came with some dessert like jelly or something else."

Then my grandpa eventually sold the flat and moved in with us. We resumed the services of this talented caterer Mrs. Martis years later when we lived in Block 2, P.E.C.H.S. What I remember is that the curries would be different for each day of the week. One day red, then green masala, then brown masala, always with rice. Side dish of beef cutlets and on Fridays awesome red fish curry with fried fish.

How the poor tiffin-wallah found his way to our house all the way from Saddar, on his bicycle, in the heat of the day is another story. My guess is that he took a short cut through Abyssinia Lines. I give full credit to this man: He had several tiffin boxes to deliver all around the area, had to pick up the empties and hand them back to Mrs. Martis in Saddar. Next day, the same routine, magically delivered on time!

Our family friend Vicki also helped me in writing this short story: She remembers Mrs. Martis very well, as they lived in the same lane in Saddar on Vincent Street (the name has changed now). It was the lane after Goa Jewellers. "Mr. and Mrs. Martis were a very hard-working couple who cooked very well. She had two sons and one daughter. They now live in the U.S.A."

A flashback from a time that has now gone by. Mrs. Martis, we still remember you and we thank you for the wonderful food, always delivered on time and FRESH! May your memory live on forever, may your family be blessed, wherever they are.

Note: The family photo is of my grandparents with their three young daughters. My mom (the youngest) was not yet born.
Photo provided by author.

'Old Garage Door'
Photo credit: Merridy Cox

Laura DeLeon

Laura DeLeon is the poet of angels, love-lore and stream of consciousness and is a spoken word artist based in Toronto. Her love of poetry, art and music are gifts that she accredits to the belief and the existence of angels. Laura has studied and received her Honors B.A in English Literature from York University. She has taught and tutored in ESL. Her moment of epiphany was when she first received her calling while working in journalism at Ryerson University. She has published a chapbook entitled, *Angels In Twilight* and a book of poems from the heart's core entitled, *Winter Be My Bride.*

COURAGE MY LOVE

Have Courage, Have Faith and for always Pray
Do not be discouraged nor dismayed
By any spirit nor thing inanimate
Object nor living being
Displaced as they may seem
By Time Immemorial unchanged
Unto life's little uncertainties
In times of calamity feel free
And try to remove the Self and the Ego
From the Evil and Wicked Doers
Who take claim on one's life
The cause of much struggle and strife
Unholy and maniacal
In Body, Mind and Soul
Undeniable in Time be known
Deceitfulness and defeatist attitude
Resist to take from the palm of the needy
And bite the hand that feeds
Give back to those who 'have not'
In want and in greed and in need
Heresay is irrelevant, not palpable
And denied in deed not word
Lest be your adorning
Speech no more to be hindered
Than the underhanded
By and by
To sew the Evil Seed of Destruction
And thus abide
To snuff out the Light of Hope
Have Courage, Have Faith and for always Pray
Your Light in the Darkness
Your Rite of Passage, your Courage, your Pathway.

INNER SYNERGY

❧

Stealing from me
My precious time
My energy of the mind
Mind fields
My time away
Synergy
Worn out, faded, toxic
Bad Faith
My Hands of the Cause
At peace, at one
Where they lay
Not corrupted, yet disrupted
Shaken
In a heartbeat
Not stolen in dismay
Yet racing with time
Free is my mind
My time on this Earth
Self-effacing
God speed you
Broken wing birds
Broken bones from within
The Soul's Light
The segregated system
Begins in deeds not words
Need not to be reminded
To be renewed
Spirits that deflect defeat
Voices silenced
Defeatist attitudes
Wills that relent
Yet in a furious fury
Evil Spirits
Backbones bent
Spinal constancy
A common place
A continuum in space

The gravity of descent
The guilty repent
To the crimes of passion
To pay heed to the Heart
And of the Mind
In passing time
The righteous and the meek
The Holy to whom retreat
To the Temple of Love
The Goddess of Sky above

Photo credit: Merridy Cox

DEAD HANDS

The contrary winds of self and passion
Change cannot affect nor alter me
Angels that appear in their midst
Grievous and almighty persist
From this tryst above
Of twisted fates in years
Finite in ruinous ways
Forever swayed by time immemorial
And sacred love

Presentiment, ingenue, inspired
Gifted guided hands that abide and admire
Regarded as still
Upon their death beds where they lay

Living in peace on the edge of time
On this precipice divine
Of earth and heavenly beings sublime
A pilgrim's kiss
So close to death
Yes, I am the one
With eyes wide open
To the sun
Fear I do surmise haunts me

For I approach my destiny
My fate in the next world to come
Free of spirit and blithe
Gifted immortal and divine
Inclined
Towards the spirit within
Towards the soul of the sun

LOVE SPEAK

❀

The mind never forgets
Nor does the body sleep
It speaks through us gently
In visions and in dreams
Carving out memory

Time is of the past
A life of transient dust
Angels on high
That must oversee
Bewail and lament
But to no avail

This plague
Be gone
This plight
This deathless flight
Be upon me
Of bygone years
In visions and in dreams

For it seems
I cannot see
Nor mirror forth
My truth
Only darkness at bay
I adhere to
My love of loves
Whilst I journey through
And sojourn
To countless other worlds
Sublime and unknown unto me.

❀

Bev Gorbet

Bev Gorbet was a pioneering teacher librarian before she began teaching language, writing and art in elementary school. She was a learning researcher with special interests in learning disability, in English as a Second Language, and in overall teaching methodologies. She wrote poetry and children's literature for over 50 years. She went on to become an advisor and advocate for issues on public education and has continued this advocacy into retirement from the classroom. She is a very proud mother and grandmother.

AND SUMMER MADE HER LIGHT ESCAPE

"Our summer made her light escape
unto the beautiful..."
~ *Emily Dickinson*

Long abides the majesty:
Worlds within worlds eternally in motion...
Summer made her light escape
And beauty fled...

We followed into golden autumn lights:
The burnished twilights of a moving world...
Then onto a silver lace purity,
Cold descent into cold winter's landscapes...

Days of windsong and bitter night storm
Soon to arrive, fertile spring airs:
All the haunted beauty, a world reborn:
Crocus and daffodil lights, lavender petal,
Rainfall days, lilac and rose...
Warm nights and lullaby breeze
High tossed, bended branch and bough...

Evensong birdcall, a landscape: horizons of promise
Tender leaf, downy petal,
Forested mosses and luminescent skies...
Azure blue, variegated green,
Soft cloud chariot gently riding on silken lights...

So abide the world, all wonder, a most glorious majesty,
Beauty bending to beauty season to tender season passing...
Time lost, memory leading:
The eternal pledge, the immortal promise....

THE MAKER OF SOULS

❀

"...is loneliness
the maker of the soul
its caverns its corridors
Illuminate or seal...?
　　~ Emily Dickinson

We grow to become in the silence of our hearts,
Beautiful soliloquy built out of solitude and longing,
the internal flame, the central vision...

So it stands, the creature alone
At the center of the universe perplexed and lost...
Soliloquy, song of heart and mind at rest...
Melody, rhythm of the best we are...

Humankind in a deepest silence, self reflection,
A deepest meditation,
A deepest contemplation,
the mind tempest-tossed and led by regret...

The soul aflame, a deepest love, a deepest discontent,
Oh! season of mists and windswept skies
Spring sweet days, the many losses, the cry...
Season of bittersweet awakenings, season of struggle,
Season of promise...

The wind and the rain will call out to us once more,
The tides again are turning,
We again face a terrible web of days,
Woven tapestries of hope and wonder...
The long journey...

Our lives will unfold day by passing day
And out of the silence grows a magnificent vision,

Heart and soul revealing, the growing, the wondrous becoming

Promises to keep...
The essential loneliness: maker and guide out of a darkest
solitude,
the profound silence to instruct and teach...
Alone to grow and become at the center of the universe...

❁

'Port Credit Lighthouse'
Photo credit: Merridy Cox

Lina Ismail Al-Hebahbeh

Lina Ismail Al-Hebahbeh immigrated to Canada from Jordan in August 2013. She is a multi-lingual storyteller. She recently published her first kids' book *Sam and his Granddad—An Alzheimer's Story*, IOWI, 2018. She holds a bachelor's degree in Physical Education and was a PE teacher and coach for various sports for kids with and without disabilities. She is currently a Peel District School Board employee.

Lina is an active volunteer with various organizations within her community and has been appointed as an ambassador of volunteer MBC organization.

'WHO ARE YOU?'—AN ALZHEIMER'S STORY

(excerpts from kids' story *Sam and his Granddad*)

❖

I spend almost every weekend with Granddad. I love spending time with him. His warm welcome made every weekend something I looked forward to all week long.

But wait… the other day I visited Granddad and he was not waiting for me by the gate like he usually did. I found him sitting on the couch in the living room and looking very tired.

"Why are you sitting here, Granddad? How come you were not by the gate waiting for me as always?" I asked worried.

"Today I feel tired… excuse me, my dear."

I wished Granddad would get well soon. I sat next to him watching TV. For the very first time, I felt bored at my Granddad's house!

And the same thing happened the next weekend… and the next. Granddad did not seem to be like he had been before. Not only was I bored sitting with him on the couch watching TV, but I also worried about him. Where was my fun-loving Granddad? Then one weekend I found him looking for his glasses while he had them on! That same day, he suddenly stopped in the middle of one of his stories and stared blankly.

"What's wrong, Granddad?" I asked in a shaking voice.

"What was I saying?" he asked.

Since then every time I visited him, I found him more different than before. He was always looking for stuff that was lying around him.

One day, when mom and I visited him, I found him very quiet, with none of the joy he showed on our previous visits. I walked towards him, but he kept staring out the window. I greeted him, but he didn't reply. I greeted him in a louder voice.

"Granddad! It's me, I've come to see you."

Then Granddad looked at me and asked: "Who are you?"

I felt so sad. Tears rose to my eyes and I ran to my mom.

"What is happening to Granddad?" I asked.

"Your Granddad suffers from Alzheimer's, my son," Mom whispered. "It is a disease that some people suffer from when they get old, like your Granddad. The disease affects their brain cells and they begin to lose their memories. They forget people, places and cannot recognize the things around them," she explained.

There was sadness in my Mom's voice as Granddad even forgot who she was.

"He is still my Granddad," I said. "And I will always love him."

"Remember your Granddad as he used to be before he became ill, son," Mom said. "Tell him you love him every chance you get."

"I will, Mom," I said, happily. "Its my turn to play with Granddad."

"I love you, Granddad."

Note: This story is based on the author's own childhood experience with a beloved grandparent who suffered with Alzheimer's

'In Cobourg'
Photo credit: Merridy Cox

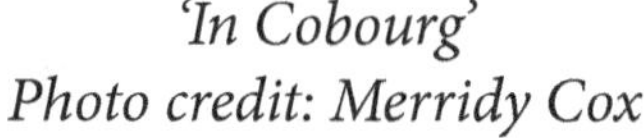

P.I. Kapllani

Përparim Kapllani (P.I.Kapllani) was born in the city of Elbasan, Albania. He immigrated to Canada in 2000, bringing with him many untold stories from his years as a journalist/military officer. He graduated as an Anti-Aircraft Gun Artillery Officer in 1990 from the University of Scanderbeg, and has a teaching degree in Literature and Albanian Language from Tirana University.

Përparim has an extensive publishing history both in Canada and his native Albania. His most recent novel is *The Thin Line*, Mawenzi House, 2018; *Genti—the king of the Ardians,* a play in Albanian, 2016; *The Last Will*, a novel based on the Çamëria genocide, IOWI, 2013; novella *The Hunter* was shortlisted by Quattro Books for The Ken Klonsky novella contest in 2015. *Beyond the Edge*—short stories, IOWI, 2010; *Queen Teuta of Illyria*—a play in English, IOWI, 2008, and in Albanian in 2014. He has published extensively in anthologies.

He is the author of five books in the Albanian language and has worked as a journalist for *Ushtria*, the Albanian Army newspaper; *Shekulli*, a daily newspaper; *Spekter* magazine and other local publications in Albania.

MEMORIES IN A NOTEBOOK

❧

Siemens AG, Convulsator!" Isa Vishanji softly read the brandname of the electroshock machine. The yellow box had a handle on top from which two electrodes extended like the two deadly tentacles of an octopus. He peered through the little glass of the wattmeter and saw that the needle had stopped at zero. A green button under the glass looked to him like the sole eye of an evil monster. He had to take note of the details and repeat the info back to himself. He believed that by repeating aloud to himself, he would commit anything to memory. It was a way to remember things, to gain knowledge—learning by rote. He would memorize even unnecessary details.

This was the third time that he had been taken to the electroshock room, even though the electroconvulsive therapy didn't seem to have any effect on him. The director of the hospital, Dr Dinçi, had himself conducted the therapy on him. His name and grave bearing heightened Isa's fear of the shock therapy. Two burly nurses held him by both arms and dragged him across the floor toward the portable bed, which was covered with a white sheet. Isa glanced down at himself. He wore white pajamas with a brown rectangular pattern and torn slippers on his feet.

He clenched his teeth tight to hold back the cry of fear that threatened to escape his dry throat. The more panic he expressed, the longer the electric shock treatment would last.

In the few seconds of relative normalcy, his life replayed backward in his mind, like a black-and-white movie. He saw the silhouette of a gray airplane travelling from Moscow. He was on a flight home after receiving a Communication Engineer's qualification. The airplane sank into cloud, but the sweet, bright face of Svjetllana was still before him, as he left Russia forever. Many Albanian students took their Russian girlfriends with them, but Svjetllana didn't want to go to Albania.

"Stay here with me," she begged him, but Isa insisted that they must live together in his homeland Albania. Since their minds were in different places, they had to break up. Svjetllana had cried all night long. She kept begging him to abandon everything and spend the rest of his life with her, but he couldn't bring himself to do that.

Since the day they broke up, he had felt lost. His mind couldn't come to terms with losing her. He had a nervous breakdown, which led him into deep depression. He had gone into his room and shut the door behind him, locking himself inside. He relived the memory of those unforgettable moments with her, when he held her in his arms.

The brilliant student Isa Vishanji had turned into a zombie who walked in his sleep through the streets of his hometown Elbasan. The brightness of Svjetllana's eyes woke him up even from the deepest dream, but she wasn't there anymore. She was thousands of kilometers away.

Isa couldn't do anything else. He didn't want to eat and he isolated himself from the rest of the world. A confusing tangle of pain and sorrow for his lost love settled like a heavy burden on his heart. The promising youth who had once won a gold medal for mathematics had transformed into the 'living dead.' He didn't speak to anyone. His father was so worried about him that he took his son to the Psychiatric Hospital of Elbasan, where Isa stayed time after time. The doctors prescribed many different kinds of antidepressants like Venlafaxine, Bupropion or Imipramine, but none of them worked.

His family couldn't accept his desperate and tragic state, especially his older sister Shpresa, who introduced him to one of her girlfriends from school. Eventually he married the friend, twenty-year-old Brunilda, with whom he had two kids.

The image of Svjetllana had faded, as the nervous breakdown took its toll. The more he tried to get rid of thoughts of her, the worse his mental state had become. Brunilda caught him with a photo of Svjetllana in his hands when he was going through a moment of high anxiety and finally asked him for a divorce. He rarely saw his kids, even though he lived in the same city as Brunilda, who was now married to someone else.

***

"Close your eyes and don't move!" Doctor Dinçi ordered him, as two nurses tied his legs and arms to both sides of the iron bed. Isa knew very well what would happen next. Doctor Dinçi would turn the knob on the electric shock machine. The electric impulses would surge through both sides of his head simultaneously. Isa had seen many patients in ward 17 during the last six months that he had been treated in this hospital. The shock therapy wasn't the best. It had side effects such as partial loss of memory.

After going through that unbearable treatment, he was supposed to get back on his feet, yet his mind struggled to bring back to his destroyed memory all the people he had loved. How could he forget the little and innocent faces of his son and daughter, Ajri and Lulja? Ajri was 10 and Lulja 7 years old. He had promised Ajri that he was going to buy him a soccer ball and for Lulja, a box of colour pencils, after he got out of the hospital. She was so eager to draw and colour and Isa wanted to support his daughter's passion for art.

"Ajri and Lulja! Ajri is my son: 'ajer' means 'air,' the air I breathe. Lulja is my daughter—the flower of the spring, who likes to draw waves on the seashore, houses, trees and animals.

"Dear son! I don't know if you will be able to understand one day how much I have suffered. Tonight, I am being treated with electro-convulsion. I am trying to forget the pain. I wish you with all my heart all the best in your life. I hope you have only joy and become educated and smart. I wish you grow up fast and become a real man. I don't know why they don't let me see you. I stare at the walls and I don't feel like doing anything. I miss you so much, my little king. The only person who understands me is Albin, the doctor on the night shift. He gave me a notebook and a pencil for good behaviour. I write down my memories and this way I keep them alive. I have hidden the notebook under the pillow. I'll write everything down, when I get back from the therapy."

Isa felt the electric current rattle his tired brain. Images crashed and folded into each other. He clung to the rubberized bars of the stretcher, as his mind spun like a turbulent whirlpool. Fragments of memory melded together. Svjetllana shook hands with his son Ajri and kissed Lulja on her rosy cheek. Brunilda laughed at him with sarcasm from the distance, as she appeared on the sidewalk beside a young and handsome man. The thunderbolt sliced the dark sky of the night, shattering it in pieces, as the approaching thunder echoed in his ears. He saw his tired body slide downwards and disappear without a trace into a black hole in space. Where had he been? His brain felt it would explode from the high pressure applied from all directions. If this treatment destroys his memory how could he live without the memories which kept him alive?

"I'll record all the details in the notebook," he promised himself and clenched his teeth against the pain. "I should not forget them. These notes will keep my memories and me alive. I'll write them down one by one!"

***

Before I went to the electroshock room. I was given some disgusting soup, which stuck in my throat. For breakfast I had just plain bread, tea and a piece of yellow cheese. The tea was chlorinated and the yellow cheese stank, which I hardly ate. I shouldn't complain, since I had seen worse. I have seen patients eating from the garbage bin. There is no rule of law behind these walls of this hospital. There is no respect for humans! When they position us in line for the morning exercise they call us not by names, but by numbers. My name is Number 12 from now on, but all of us are called by one collective name: "The Animals!" Last night three "patients" entered my room and beat the hell out of me. They hit me with the legs of a broken table and kicked me nonstop. I fought back to defend myself as much as I could. Once I thought to jump from the fifth floor, but then I remembered the windows up there are also fitted with iron bars.

How is it that there are so many bad people around, people with no soul? I can hardly breathe and my back hurts. Ufff! I think they induced me into having more seizures. I want to tell the doctors: Please, take these electrodes off my head, since you are not going to cure me. I am afraid that I am going to die without being able to see you for the last time, son!

They gave me an injection in my arm and put me to sleep. I don't know how long I slept. When I woke up, I noticed that I was in handcuffs. An intelligence officer stood in front of me. He said he was 'Fatmir.' He had a mustache and large reading glasses. His military uniform hugged his body, and he lashed his fine boots with a whip. He asked me how I know Svjetllana Konstandinova. I didn't tell them before that Svjetllana was my Russian girlfriend. Perhaps I had mentioned her name in delirium and now they are using it against me. This officer with the name 'Fatmir' accused me of being a secret agent of the KGB! -The Russain intelligence agency. How can I be an agent, when it was me who won a gold medal and chose to come back to my country above all? Definitely it has been a misunderstanding and I believe that they will get me out of this hospital-jail. Hope dies last, not the soul. Soon I will join you, son!

***

Isa Vishanji opened his eyes and gazed tiredly around the room. The shock therapy had ended and the doctors had taken him back to his room, where five more patients were accommodated. Six patients in one tiny room. His body was numb and his bones felt broken, but the shock therapy didn't have the results that they were expecting. The shocks couldn't destroy his memories. Svjetllana,

Shpresa, Brunilda, Ajri, Lulja, Albini… all the people out there with whom he managed to have some kind of relationship—their names were written down on the yellow pages of his notebook. He caressed it and hid it under the pillow and laughed triumphantly. He had pieces of memories that they would never destroy.

*Author's note: *This story is based on the true life of my father I. Kapllani, who underwent treatment for mental illness. In February 1977, he was found dead in a street in Elbasan, Albania, at the age of 43 years.*

'Old Government Building in Kingston'
Photo credit: Merridy Cox

Lillian Khan

Lillian Khan is originally from India and now calls Canada her home. Coming from a family of educators, she believes in learning for life. A former marketing consultant, she is currently a licensed payroll compliance practitioner. In her first collection of poems, *Soulfie—set your free*, In Our Words Inc., 2017, she presents her journey through life from a soul perspective. For more info on the works of Lillian Khan, visit: soulpoetess.com

HOPE

Sunrise follows sunset,
dusk follows dawn...
So when your heart is breaking,
know that there's a new morn.

Every breath you take,
carries new hope alive.
So let the past be buried,
don't rattle the corpses inside.

Everything that happens,
is for the greater good.
Even if it your life threatens,
or is wrapped in falsehood.

Nature gives us clues,
that gifts in the shell hide.
Remove the outer layers,
and delve into the surprise.

Nothing is as it seems,
forge through the heart-ache and broken dreams.
Claim your treasure, yourself redeem.
Keep hope in your heart alive!

LETTERS TO MY CHILDREN

Fill the earth with your laughter, love and caring,
don't be dismayed,
with folks that are hard and unwavering.
Be kind to those who need it most,
heed your soul's guidance.
When I'm gone,
don't run from pillar to post.

Be the champion of the under-dog.
The beggar, the down-trodden,
the sick, the seniors
and those whose minds are in a fog.
Remember those that the world has forgot,
bring a smile to their lips,
don't let their souls and bodies rot.

Remember to always wipe the tears,
of those whose hearts are breaking,
are weary and laden with burdens and fears.
Be passionate, compassionate,
not rude and obstinate.
Even though that may be the trend.
Lend a helping hand,
to those who need a friend.

My darling children, if you remember and follow this,
I can rest in peace, in happiness and bliss,
as you are my living legacy to the world,
I live through you,
In your actions and words.

PARALLEL REALITIES

Parallel realities,
choices made,
culminating fantasies.
Like takes on a camera,
each shot different,
not connected.
Another path,
another life,
unrelated.

What if's,
gawking and leering,
along the way.
A different choice,
could have resulted in another array.
But somewhere desire set momentum in motion,
parallel realities,
as abundant, as drops in the ocean.

Phyllis Kwan

Phyllis Kwan was born in Trinidad, West Indies, and came to Canada with her family in 1969. She attended school in Toronto and went to Ryerson Polytechnic Institute. She has run a family drycleaning business since 1986, helping make it a consistently strong contender for business excellence. Phyllis' close-knit family has inspired much of her writing. Her first collection of poetry is *Poetic Ballets of my Mind*, In Our Words Inc., 2016.

Phyllis lives in Cabbagetown, Toronto, with her husband of 40 years, and close to her adored two children and two grandsons.

THEN & NOW: KEEPING A PROMISE

❖

"Then" refers to the years 1967 and 2012, two years when I made a promise to Saint Anthony of Padua that if he were to help me find my lost treasured items, then I would visit his shrine in Padua and light a candle in homage to him. I found my lost treasures on both occasions.

"Now" is the year 2018 when I felt the urge to keep those promises. I finally visited the little town of Padua in Italy with my husband Steve on Monday, July 30. The benefit of this trip which enabled me to keep my promise to Saint Anthony is that my husband and I were both able to check off some of our bucket list items in life. And to be able to do it at this time in our lives in style and comfort added to the pleasure and sense of adventure.

It was a magical adventure. Keeping my promise made years ago led to a wonderful vacation in Europe creating unforgettable memories.

The first of our dreams to be realized on this trip was the Sound of Music tour in Salzburg. This had been a dream of mine since 1965 when I first saw the movie as a little girl. It made a huge impression on me and shaped my life to a certain degree. I consciously, and subconsciously, tried to be as good a person as I imagined Maria von Trapp to be. I strove to always be kind, good, fun, honest, truthful, adventurous and brave as I was growing up. I knew all the words to all of the songs having seen the movie about a hundred times. What a treat to be able to see the real-life venue of one of my favourite movies!

From Salzburg, Austria to Padua, Italy, a drive of about seven hours, Steve realized his bucket list dream of driving super fast. We had rented a sleek Audi A6 and he reached a speed of 242 kph on the A4 highway from Austria to Italy. It was exhilarating, and I had to marvel at his skill and superb control. I imagined that was what it would feel like to be seated beside Mario Andretti, the famous race car driver, as we sped along the A4 highway southbound toward our destination of

Padua. I was so proud of his skillful driving and total control at all times. It was impressive to just be there by his side living this experience with him.

We went directly to the Basilica of St. Anthony. On July 30, I was able to touch the marble crypt of St. Anthony. The marble felt very cold to my hand on a very, very hot summer's day in Italy. I am unsure if I imagined it, but I felt a slight jolt of energy as I touched the crypt of the saint. It was surreal. And I immediately felt a sense of relief and happiness that I was finally able to keep this promise I made years ago, first as a young girl in 1967 and secondly as a mature woman in 2012. I felt deep satisfaction.

After spending another two days in Padua, we continued on our tour through Europe. On our final night we dined at the Charles Lindbergh restaurant. While dining there, we were entertained by a very talented guitarist and singer, Armin. His exceptional musical talent made the evening magical and I applauded enthusiastically. For his last number at 10 pm, which was when the staff at the restaurant began preparing to close, Armin announced he was dedicating his final song of the evening to me. He sang Ed Sheeran's 'Perfect' and indeed, the night and our magical vacation ended on a perfect note. A celebration of our 40 years of marriage and especially the satisfaction of being true to a vow taken so many years ago.

Keeping a promise:
The author in Italy.

'Deadwood Silhouette'
Photo credit: Merridy Cox

Susan Munro

Susan Munro is a poet, holistic healer and life-time student of the esoteric arts. Born and raised in Toronto, she has lived in Alberta and Phoenix, Arizona, which allowed her some different perspectives. She now lives permanently in Toronto and provides sanctuary to a number of furry companions. She has written two books of poetry, *Coil* in 2012 and *Ravings of a Lunatic Saint* in 2013. Her passions are advocating for those that cannot speak and her poetry is all about her musings and observations regarding life, love and the extreme mystery of it all.

GRATITUDE

It was not too long ago
I still believed in white knights
puppy dog tails
wishing on a falling star

Maturity is not cynicism
nor is it a heavy weight of resignation
Comes carried on Wisdom
Opening of the inner eye

No need to carry burdens
of resentment or hurt
freed from the chains of want
to rest in the glory of gratitude

Breathing, eyes opening in morning
a sunset of glorious iridescent gold
crispness of a winter morning
beat of a heart, fading into sleep

I need so little
    but always wanted so much

IT MATTERS

I weep for the tuskless elephant
the hornless Rhino
the finless shark

I am despaired by the care-less
the heart-less
the soul-less

It matters

I see vacant eyes
staring into phones
with headsets to shut out the rest

I see killings and maimings
I see children harmed by vaccines
governments covering it up

It matters

I see the homeless starving
on city streets
bereft of care

I see the aged not eating
or living vacuously
in a home not a home

It matters

Drugs are the new Gods
we pay homage to
while our minds rot

Children not allowed
to be children
only supervised chattel

It matters

Voices are being raised
the world throughout
a unison of revolt

Taxes overwhelming
backs breaking
spirits broken

It matters… more than ever

'Kildeer family'
Photo credit: Merridy Cox

Lovina D'Souza

Lovina D'Souza is a passionate photographer and writer. Originally from India, she also loves travelling and seeing the world through her 'special lens.' Her hobby of photography turned into a business with encouragement from family and friends and today 'Photographer La Vie' is a sought-after professional photography option, particularly within the Goan (South Asian) community. Photographer La Vie specializes in wedding and special event photography, as well as individual and family portraits and corporate/product shots.

Lovina spends much of her leisure time volunteering in her community. She believes in living a simple and balanced life. To see her portfolio, visit: http://photographerlavi.wixsite.com/lavi

My mother, my inspiration. Lovina D'Souza's mother Emilda Rodricks and her brother Franklin Rodricks, then and now.

Akemi Tomoda

Akemi Tomoda came to Canada in 1970 from her native Japan, following her marriage to husband Ken. She did not speak English at the time. In the years since, she has studied English and art, particularly watercolour painting. She is a devout Christian and regularly journals her 'testimony' of God's blessings in her life. She published *Akemi's Journal*, 2011, which has been translated into Japanese. She continued to write as a form of healing and gratitude and published *Akemi's Journal 2*, In Our Words Inc., 2017. She lives in Mississauga, where she is busy with her favourite hobbies of gardening, sewing and Bible study.

SURVIVAL THROUGH WRITING

❀

I was born in a little village in Japan before World War II. My father was a school teacher, and his family believed in Buddhism for many generations, and my mother was a daughter of a Shinto priest. We experienced hardship and food shortage during World War II, but we managed quite well, and I was a happy child.

After I graduated from teacher's college I started to suffer from depression. At first it wasn't a big problem, but it became deeper and deeper and I did not want to live any more. I read so many books to find an answer to my problem, but I could not find any. During this time, I came across a tiny book *For the Sleepless Night* written by Carl Hilty. He wrote nothing but God's love and friendship with Jesus Christ, which I did not understand at all. But one sentence from his book touched my heart deeply. He wrote "If you feel like shooting yourself in the head with a gun, read a Bible instead; and if you want to hang yourself with a rope, go to a church instead." I wanted to be free from depression so badly that I tried it. I started going to a church by riding a bicycle for 15 minutes and taking a train to the next city and walked about 30 minutes, because there wasn't a Christian church in our little village and there were no Christians. After a couple of years of struggle, I finally became a Christian in the year 1965. I was baptized in a little church in Mikara.

I met Ken Tomoda in the early spring of 1970 in Japan while he was on vacation from Canada to visit his family. We exchanged many letters and I decided to come to Canada to marry him in the fall of 1970. We lived in North York for several years and later moved to Mississauga.

After several years of prayers, my husband became a Christian, and we read the Bible together and prayed together. We enjoyed beautiful times together. In 2000, one beautiful sunny Saturday morning he passed away suddenly from a massive heart attack.

That moment everything changed. I was overwhelmed by the grief of my husband's death and worries about my future living in a foreign country without a husband and children. I could not eat anything for two and a half weeks and shed tears every day for more than three months. I just cried and cried, and one day I said to God with tears, "Lord, I can't live like this. Help me! If you fail to help me, I can't survive."

God responded to my request by sending many kind people into my life. God also helped me and healed me through writing of essays. My English teacher, Eleanore Sproule visited me and taught me English even before my husband's death. After my husband's death, I could not think of anything, so I stopped taking English lessons, but I resumed it after a few months. Every time Eleanore visited me I presented one essay. This helped me to go through the most difficult time in my life. I tried to see something good in my life instead of difficulties. I trained my mind to see something good in everything and learned the importance of thanksgiving in my life.

God healed me with watercolour painting. My husband loved art so much and he introduced me to art. He took me to New York, Chicago, Buffalo, Ottawa and Toronto to visit art galleries. After his death, I started taking art classes at Visual Arts Mississauga and found such joy in painting. When I paint, I lose myself completely in painting and nothing bothers me anymore.

God healed me through gardening. Ken left quite a big garden in my backyard. It was his garden and I did not touch it at all. But after his sudden death I had to look after the garden by myself. Right after I watered the garden for the first time I cried out to God, "Lord help me. I have to look after the garden by myself now. Send me someone who can help me to look after the garden." Then two hours later, Phyllis, a lady who lived on our street, brought a young man to my home and said, "Akemi, this is Gary. He wants to help you." Then Gary said, "I am your gardener." I cried. Since then, Gary has helped me in the garden and in the house too. He helped me a lot and I really thanked God for that.

In the year 2001, one Sunday in early summer I came home from church and opened the living room door to go out into the garden, and God spoke to me. "Thank you for looking after my garden." I was shocked and could not move for a long time. Since then I started calling my backyard "The Lord's Garden" and I started sensing the peace of God and enjoyed it so much.

Years have passed since my husband's death. God has helped and healed me all these years. I did not become an angry or bitter person. I am so thankful for that. I am still writing about the goodness of God in my life, and I thank God every time I write.

This page and facing page: watercolour paintings by Akemi Tomoda of 'The Lord's Garden'

Anna Yin

Born in China, **Anna Yin** immigrated to Canada in 1999. She has authored six poetry books including *Seven Nights with the Chinese Zodiac*, Black Moss, 2015, and *Inhaling the Silence*, Mosaic Press, 2013. Anna has won many awards including the 2005 Ted Plantos Memorial Award, the 2010/2014 MARTY Literary Arts Awards and three OAC awards. Her poems and translations have appeared in numerous publications including the *New York Times*, *Arc Poetry*, *CBC Radio*, *Rogers TV*, *China Daily*, *World Journal*, *Poetry in Transit*.

Anna was appointed Mississauga's Inaugural Poet Laureate (2015-2016) and currently teaches Poetry Alive in schools and colleges. Her website is annapoetry.com

LUCKY DAYS
–after Marty Gervais

They call you
a lucky girl.
Nobody knows
you are careful
to pinch
your own luck
– not too much of it,
or else you must fall in the dark.

You often dream of a black cat
but wake up to catch
a glimpse of a self –
irises so bright,
eager to jump out.

You admit your blessing –
to retreat to shadows in time…
turning into a shadow maker,
not a moth toward fire.

The unknown remains unknown.
Sirens shatter Gwendolyn's dream.
With luck, a life you know –
the way of Poetry.

Note: "Shadow Maker" is the title of Rosemary Sullivan's biography of poet Gwendolyn MacEwen.

AT THE WRONG PARTY

Entering the room,
I found no one I knew.
Among well-suited strangers,
in a rose dress from a bargain basement
I, naively bright, like a crystal figurine.
Guests spoke in a foreign lingo,
haiku slipped from my tongue,
dropped, cracked, then crashed
on their gold-grounded topics,
greasily attached to green notes.
The host nodded, his fingers
raised, declaring his bids.
Others cheered: five, all
profitable estates,
two in Washington,
three in New York.
How about you? they turned
to ask, pity in their eyes,
as they saw my bare hand,
nix, disapproval…
Shattered, I let my heart cry:
we are all broken, stripped
down from rising heights
to the flattened earth.
I, this useless poet
with paper robe;
they, the wrong party
with gold-diving gravity.

A Compass Rose

In my heart,
there is always a space
for a rose.
Whenever I am in the dark,
I plant one, a tiny bud.
It becomes my hope.
Soon its light fills in
this little spot,
then the whole sky,
and becomes thorns
to those who are playing blind.
I hear their mourning,
I see their paleness.
Teach me how to plant
one for them,
but do not ask me
to bury my own.

Liana Di Marco

Liana C. Di Marco, B.A., M.E.S., is a published multi-media artist, writer, teacher and musician. Liana's art work is a collection to match her writing on various themes ranging from survival, free-speech, justice, faith and hope. Each art piece is a window to a chapter in her life. Each written word is a reflective thought.

MOVIN' ON

Yesterday is done
Tomorrow awaits
Today I do

Hand in hand
With God I go
No live band
No music flow

In thought I ponder
All purpose deep
Nothing beyond yonder
Hefty price not cheap

Step by step I walk
The path is hard
I listen to all talk
A spade is not my card

Yesterday is back
Tomorrow is done
Today I dance

Norma Nicholson

Norma Nicholson, BA, MA is a three-time published author, speaker, educator, youth and adult mental health advocate. She is a retired registered nurse, with a BA in Sociology and Psychology from the University of Toronto, and an MA in Adult Education from Central Michigan University, USA. She is a part-time professor at Sheridan College, and has managed health care in a variety of hospital sectors, community care access centre and provincial secure youth custody. She has held senior positions on the boards of several community organizations in the Peel region, including the Registered Nurses' Association (Peel and Ontario) and is currently the Chair of the Peel Police Services Board.

She is the author of three books, two memoirs, *Young Lives on the Line: You can make and difference* and *Walking Miles in Sensible Shoes: A nurse looks back at her vocation,* and a kids' book, *Canada My Furever Home: Codi's Adventures.*

Norma has received numerous awards for mentorship and community engagements, most recent are the Rose Fortune Award from the Ontario Black History Society; Leading Women Building Community from the Ontario Legislature; Lifetime Achievement in Nursing from the Region of Peel RNAO Chapter.

A TAP ON THE SHOULDER

✤

The rewards for those who persevere far exceed the pain that must precede the victory...Ted Engstrom

I worked as a nanny in a household of five, but hung onto my dream of becoming a registered nurse. I knew I needed to save to afford nursing school and so I worked fulltime as a nanny and spent my two days off each week to volunteer in an acute care children's hospital. I observed the positive impact that nurses had on the lives of their patients and families, and I wanted to serve in such a role.

I daydreamed during my volunteer hours about my future career and sponged up all the information I could find on nursing. When I applied to nursing college, I was informed that I needed to have completed grade 13 Mathematics. So, I switched categories to become a Registered Practical Nurse.

I studied part-time and took a casual job to have time to study. I studied hard and passed all requirements including the Provincial exams to become certified in Ontario and gained employment in the same hospital where I had volunteered— without the need of an interview!

Many times I wished that I could become a registered nurse. I had gained so many skills over eight years as an RPN that I was called on to support newly hired registered nurses during their orientation. My enhanced skills allowed me to provide high levels of care, but I was prohibited from doing so because of the guidelines for my RPN practice. A registered nurse was allowed to deliver medications by intravenous to children; but I was only allowed to give medication orally.

Then one day things changed. I was assigned to a patient care unit where on that particular tour of duty there were 12 infants and 16 toddlers, all between the ages of six months to two years. There were three RPNs and one RN on duty to deliver care to this large number of children. I so wished that I could use roller blades to get around but had to be content with wearing running shoes.

As I made my rounds to see my eight *little* patients at the beginning of my tour of duty, I observed that Johnny's intravenous tube inserted into his left wrist was almost empty! I did not have the option of waiting for the RN to do this due to the immediate need to hang a new bag of fluids. The RN was unavailable for ten minutes.

The registered nurse had prepared bags of intravenous fluids for each patient and labeled them very clearly with their names and room numbers. For easy access, these were placed in a cupboard above each patient's bed/crib. I reached into the cupboard, took out the intravenous fluid that belonged to Johnny, doubled checked the label against the infant's arm bracelet, removed the empty bag, hung the new one and ensured an effective flow of fluids into the infant's wrist. I felt so proud that I prevented a restart of an IV for such a small infant where it is often very difficult to find a vein.

I was just about to leave the infant's room to inform the RN of what I did, when I felt a tap on my shoulder. I was so engaged in what I had accomplished that I did not hear the footsteps of the evening supervisor as she entered the room.

She said, "What do you think you are doing, young lady? You must know by now that only an RN is allowed to change intravenous bags on patients." I explained why I did the task and reassured her that I was on my way to ask the RN to come to double check that everything was okay. She responded, "When you return to work tomorrow evening, go directly to the nursing administration department before going on duty."

I was so scared, I ran to find the registered nurse to inform her not only about the infant's intravenous but what the supervisor had said. I felt that I would lose my job because of what I did to help the infant. I barely slept that night.

I went to work earlier that evening so that I could get to the administration department prior to going on duty. The evening supervisor met me at the front desk and then welcomed me into her office. There I saw the Vice President of Nursing and my manager awaiting my arrival, I was sure that this was not good news. My manager spoke first and informed me that she received wonderful feedback from the supervisor about my work ethics. I felt my heart slow, my headache diminish! I asked what she was told but instead of responding, she asked, *"Do you want to become a registered nurse?"*

I could not believe what I was hearing! Instead of saying yes, I said I could not because of a lack of finances. The supervisor then informed me that this was not the first time she had heard about my work ethic and having seen my dedication for herself, she had recommended to the Vice President that the hospital support me with an education fund to obtain my RN diploma. There were no words to express my happiness on hearing such an offer. Lots of happy tears flowed!

I accepted gracefully and signed a contract, which requested that after graduation and successful completion of my provincial examination, I would return to work in the capacity of a registered nurse for a minimum of three years. Who could ever say no to such an offer.

Many blessings came my way: I accepted and enrolled into the Nursing Diploma program at George Brown College, my tuition and books were paid by the hospital. I had access to the medical library to aid my studies, networked with many colleagues who mentored me through the three years of study and received an Ontario grant to pay other bills. What more could a person ask for except to give thanks and ensure successful completion of my studies.

After three years of study, I graduated as the Valedictorian of my class and successfully completed my Provincial RN examinations. I had immediate employment at the hospital that supported me financially, physically and emotionally. I remember reading a column in the daily news written by Ann Landers where she said that opportunities are usually disguised as hard work, so most people don't recognize them. I worked hard for the opportunity I was given and pledged to myself to be successful.

After 46 years working as a registered nurse, I am now an author, public speaker, educator and advocate for marginalized children and their families. Life surprises me each and every day, but that day, a turning point in my life, it began with a tap on the shoulder.

Patrick Njoku

Patrick Njoku was born in Nigeria but left his homeland some time after its devastating Civil War to study writing, Greek, and business studies at Aristotle University in Thessaloniki, Greece. In 1985, he came to Canada where he met his wife Geraldine and raised a family of three sons and eventually a granddaughter, his 'Princess Nayeli.'

Retired after a successful career in the pharmaceutical industry, he began reflecting on his experiences and observations growing up in the rich Igbo culture of pre-Civil War Nigeria and during the war itself. In 2018, he published his first book *My Mother's Wife* which is fictional, yet firmly rooted in his own family history. It is the first book in a planned trilogy.

... AND OBI CAME HOME!
excerpt from a short story

Obi had taken the bush path many times in the past while running errands for his parents. He took this route more often than the regular paved road, because it was a short-cut. His mother often said to him, "*son, the shortest way home is not always the safest.*" But for young Obi, this route offered an irresistible chance at adventures among the shades and sounds of the large Iroko and Obeche trees and the strange birds that nested there. This evening it was getting late when Obi set off.

Young boys like Obi were groomed to be brave, not afraid of the dark or lonely pathways, for the people believed that ancestral spirits guarded and guided them.

This thought was playing through young Obi's mind as he trotted along, sometimes breaking into a run. The night was so dark, with a threatening rainstorm, with flashes of distant lightening across the vast dark night sky. His father had told him years ago that if he ever felt afraid on dark nights, along lonely pathways, he should have a pretend-conversation with an imaginary companion. He told him that the sound of his voice reverberating in his ears would chase the fear away and give him courage to continue. He had said to his son, *fear is an interior attack by a false evidence appearing real. The spirits use their invisible state to frighten us, but if you learn how to counter it, you will not be afraid of them. We are spirits ourselves.*

Obi recalled his father's words from yester-years because suddenly he felt the hairs on the back of his neck doing an eerie ruffling. At a point he thought he really heard a voice in the bushes whispering his name...*Obi, Obi where are you going in the dark?* Then, he felt a hand touching the back of his left shoulder. Employing his father's advice, he yelled out loud at the invisible being: "*Shut up and hurry up, we are running late.*" He felt a surge of courage and felt tall and bolder and began whistling.

The relief was short-lived, for there was an actual hand gripping his shoulder menacingly as if it meant to rip his left arm off his shoulder. He broke into cold sweat, and it dawned on him that his motivational self-talk didn't work.

Obi was shocked that the voices sounded familiar, but in his confused state of mind he couldn't put a finger on it. He struggled in vain to make out those voices and call out their names. He knew that the wizardry of kidnapping loses its validity once the name(s) of the kidnappers are called out.

The kidnappers had thrown a dark scarf over his head and blindfolded him. He tried to peer through to see their faces. He tried to stay alert. His captors led him away to an unknown destination. They half-dragged, half-carried him in a zigzag path through the bush to disorient him. He tried to locate the big Iroko tree at the center of their village square. The distant sound of a crowing rooster made him realize that they were near a compound of one of the neighboring hamlets. Since he couldn't hear the pounding of grains in a wooden mortar and pestle, which would have been a sure sign of mothers preparing evening meals for their families, his disorientation increased. Obi started to panic. He, Obi, the son of the brave Nwadike, his father, was afraid!

After what seemed like eternity from the point of his abduction, his abductors took him into the barn in a compound. He knew this from the smell of goat and other domestic animals' droppings. There was no sound of children playing. Obi felt the dampness of the enclosure where they put him. It must have been a place where they stored yams and cocoa yams for the famine seasons. His head was exploding with the question of: "*what do they want to do with me? My father is not wealthy, so they couldn't be expecting to be paid a ransom.*"

He recalled the history lessons he was taught at school on how the slave trade was practiced here in west Africa. His father told him the story that was handed down from their ancestors. Some of the stories sounded like fairytales.

One story was that the father of the family in a polygamous household would bring out bags of cowries and make the children count out the cowries into hundred pieces per group. Any lazy counter became a possible commodity to be sold out to the slave traders.

Obi's heart sank, but he tried to reason with this fear. *That was during slavery days, this is today, Nigeria and neighbouring Ghana have both gained independence from their colonial masters.* Were they going to butcher him for food? *But people in West African villages today are not starving, why would they eat human flesh?*

Another fear then gripped Obi. *Would they sell him for a ritual sacrifice?* This story was rife `in Nigeria and Ghana. The unfortunate captive would be sold to a buyer who would invoke the spirit of wealth.

"Why me!" he yelled, not minding if his captors would hear. They did hear and came running armed with very sharp looking machetes.

Obi said to himself *I am not going to die a coward. I am going to make a run for it. My father's name is Nwadike (the son of the brave one), and that is how I will die.*

His captors hadn't thought that a twelve-year-old lad had a chance of escaping from them and had not secured him other than putting him in a cage. The darkness was their security. Where would he run to in a dark African jungle? He would know that wild animals were there.

 Obi's blindfold was getting loose as they never bothered to check to see if it was secure. He never asked them questions. They were sure he'd been fully disoriented by the way they took him. This was another successful job.

They approached the holding cage with the machetes, not planning on using them. They just wanted to scare him, they wouldn't kill him…their 'business' would be a failure if they did.

Obi had planned to die or escape, which ever came first he would take it gladly. When they opened the cage, he waved his hand in front of him as a blind person would when trying to feel his way out.

"What do you want?" the leader of the pack asked him.

"I want to go to the latrine, I am badly pressed." They looked at each other having not anticipated such a request. He sounded subdued and defeated. Obi feigned tiredness and extreme exhaustion after the night's ordeal.

"Sure thing, you may poo right where you are and clean yourself with your shirt," said one of them.

"Are you out of your mind," interjected another member of the gang. "If Ogah sniffs any foul smell on him, he is going to cut our money. Let somebody take him to the back house and wait for him to do his business and bring him back here. No-one would run off in that dark jungle."

Obi heard them talking praying that they would take him to the back house to do his business.

"Okay come out," barked the one sent to take him.

He took off the blindfold and made a run for the bushes at the back house. His guard was very sure that he would not dare attempt an escape. But there he was wrong.

Obi ran blindly like a gazelle that is being chased by a hungry lion. Just as his guard realized what had happened, there was a loud clap of thunder followed by torrential rain.

Obi ran blindly, not knowing where he was headed. All he planned to do was to get as far away from his captors as possible. He ran as if he had wings and felt that he was flying. The bushes were as clear to him as in daylight. Obi ran and ran. He tasted the salty frosts coming out of his mouth and nostrils. Obi ran, oh how he ran! He ran for dear life. He ran non-stop until the first crow of the cock. He never stopped once to rest.

He wondered fleetingly if he was still alive or had become one of the spirits of folklore his parents had told him about.

As dawn broke, he feared his captors would follow him. He thought if he ran in the daytime, he would attract suspicion, so he walked like the homeless children begging for alms on streets and in village markets. At night he kept running. The landscapes were getting more and more familiar as he wound his way towards his home. At some point he joined some kids doing labour on local mud-hut construction. They were not paid, just given food and drink.

Three weeks after his disappearance, his parents and sister thought he was lost, either torn to shreds by some wild animals or caught and sold as ritualistic sacrifice. His mother Grace hated the day she sent Obi on that errand three weeks ago. She had warned him several times never to take that bush path, but Obi always wanted to prove that he was capable of handling himself in the face of any danger. He was sure of his tireless running stamina. But Obi never bargained for what befell him that day.

Nwadike, his father, for some reason was sure that Obi would walk through the door any day soon. Each time his friends visited to console him and his wife, he told them: "My boy is not lost, he is going to walk through that door soon." In the privacy of his room, Nwadike cried bitter tears. He hated any kind of pity. He was always consoling people who visited him to have faith, "my boy is not lost, he is coming home soon."

On the twenty-fourth day of Obi's disappearance, as early as five-thirty in the morning, the family dog started barking furiously. Nwadike, came out and called out to his dog to be quiet. But the dog's barking sounded welcoming! Nwadike glanced over and saw his beloved Obi lunging exhausted towards his compound. He let out a loud jubilant cry: *My Boy Obi is home! He is alive!*

The whole village erupted with the sound of jubilation.

Grace, his mother, and Ada, his sister, fell on Obi's neck and hugged and kissed him non-stop. For four continuous days, the celebration went on in Nwadike's compound. Friends and relatives came from all over.

Obinna Nwadike had come back from the dead.

'On the Don East Trail'
Photo credit: Merridy Cox

Zohra Zoberi

Zohra Zoberi is a writer and producer, who has published in numerous Canadian and U.S. anthologies. She has won Literary and Performing Arts Awards from the Government of Canada, Mississauga Arts Council and other organizations, including the Woman's Courage award and Ambassador of Peace award. In her writing, she has addressed issues of cyberbullying, arranged marriages, rising divorce rates, sexual harassment and murdered/missing Indigenous women.

For 35 years of continued service to the community, she is recognized by IAOTP (International Association of Top Professionals) as 2018's Top Artistic Director of a non-profit organization, Bridging the Gap Productions, whose slogan is ***Enlightenment through Entertainment***.

HAZEL INSPIRATION
based on the 2012 artistic tribute by the Pakistani community

As I gazed at the artistic tribute
presented by my community
to honour our Legendary mayor
It took me back three decades plus!

In 1978
A new immigrant,
I was excited yet apprehensive:
'Would I achieve success in this country'?
The most welcome news at the time was:
"Hazel McCallion elected as the Mayor of Mississauga."
Who knew what a role model for us all
she would turn out to be!

In 1979
On November 10th
a train derailed, poisonous gases escaped
our bustling city became a ghost town!
Fearful citizens had to be evacuated but ...
Fearless Hazel and her team took control
A sprained ankle did not deter the determined
Hazel, who visited the site herself and
continued to hobble to press conferences.
Acknowledged around the world as
the most orderly evacuation in history—
of 200,000 residents!

In 1998
I was experiencing a burnout but...
'Our Hazel remained steadfast,' I reflected
A drastic career change I dared
After two successful decades
in the world of finance (CIBC)

I felt liberated.
I discovered
Unlimited opportunities our city offered

In 2008
Arts Council Awards Gala
as the guest of honour
McCallion literally danced her way to Stage West
to pay tribute to the winning artists.
One of the recipients myself, yet I couldn't help reflect:
'How small are my humble contributions
in comparison'!

Power to Hazel
Elected and re-elected
year after year, uncontested.
The world's 'Second Best Mayor' once.
Not a Feminist, yet a strong advocate
of women's rights.
Founder of 'Hazel's Hope'

Author Zohra Zoberi with former Mississauga mayor Hazel McCallion (photo supplied by author)

McCallion continued to inspire others

In 2012
Thirty-three years down the road
for her it was still uphill
from my office window I watched
the City Centre, its impressive skyline.
From a small collection of towns
and villages like Streetsville,
to become one of Canada's largest
the City of Mississauga—
no longer 'just a bedroom community.'
How she has spearheaded the development
of a 'downtown' where
Art, culture and architecture so thrive.
Celebration Square bustles with activity
in our 'debt free' city.

So, thank you
For enhancing the land of the Anishinaabe.
You may not know McCallion
that you have been my Hazel inspiration.

www.ingramcontent.com/pod-product-compliance
Lightning Source LLC
Chambersburg PA
CBHW071940210726
48293CB00004BA/1302